Reimagining

Writing

Assessment

Reimagining

Writing

Assessment

From Scales to Stories

MAJA WILSON

Foreword by Thomas Newkirk

HEINEMANN
Portsmouth, NH

Heinemann
361 Hanover Street
Portsmouth, NH 03801–3912
www.heinemann.com

Offices and agents throughout the world

The author and publisher wish to thank those who have generously given permission to reprint borrowed material:

Excerpt from blog entry "Use Formative Assessment as Your Classroom Fitbit" by Kathy Dyer, posted September 24, 2015, on *Teach. Learn. Grow. The Education Blog:* http://www.nea.org/blog/2015/use-formative-assessment -as-your-classroom-fitbit/. Used by permission of Northwest Evaluation Association (NWEA).

Cataloging-in-Publication Data is on file at the Library of Congress.
ISBN: 978-0-325-07478-8

Editor: Thomas Newkirk
Production editor: Patty Adams
Typesetter: Gina Poirier Design
Cover and interior designs: Suzanne Heiser
Manufacturing: Steve Bernier

Printed in the United States of America on acid-free paper

21   20   19   18   17   VP   1   2   3   4   5

To Tom Newkirk.

It's been a great privilege to work with you.

Contents

Acknowledgments

My gratitude to three teachers at Asa Adams Elementary School: Megan Dreher, Kim Oldenburgh, and Tiffany Twitchell. Many of the ideas in this book emerged through our conversations and collaborations. Megan, I'm particularly thankful for the work our classes did together. I learned much from your patience, and, of course, from your students.

I couldn't have written this book without the compositions of Miranda, Betsy, "Bob," Micah, Jonah, and Ben. I'm lucky to have been some small witness to the stories of your growth.

Citations throughout this book don't do justice to the influence that these teachers and scholars have had on my thinking: Peter Elbow, Linda Rief, Katie Wood Ray, Chris Gallagher, Tom Newkirk, Donald Murray, Penny Kittle, Bob Broad, and Tom Romano. A special thanks to Richard Haswell and Janis Haswell. We've never met, but you've practiced a beautiful kind of hospitality with me.

Thanks to the good people at Heinemann—Edie Davis Quinn, Margaret LaRaia, Suzanne Heiser, and Patty Adams—for your expertise and efforts. I'm grateful Heinemann has taken a chance on another book that pushes against the grain.

I'll never forget Gloria Pipkin, who got this whole thing started over a decade ago.

Thanks also to my dad. Your voice is often in my head while I write.

And a final thanks to Chris and Chewbacca. Our conversations—along with your suggestions, patience, and companionship—have been a gift.

Foreword by Thomas Newkirk

*a*bout a month ago, with too much time on my hands, I checked the Amazon rating for my book, *The Art of Slow Reading*. Then, just for the hell of it, I wondered how I stacked up with one of the great classics—so I checked out *King Lear*. And I actually beat out *Lear* by a couple of tenths. This result might be explainable by the fact that my book is considerably more upbeat than *Lear*—no dead daughters or gouging out of eyes. Or perhaps what I offer is more practical than *Lear*, which really delivers only some fairly oblique advice about parenting and kingship.

Of course, we are probably talking about different readers. And of course, if we could have corralled all of these readers into one of those calibration sessions, we might come to some agreement about excellence and significance, which would have placed *Lear* in its proper ascendency. Maybe. Or it could be that assessment is so variable that any attempt to bring it to uniformity is transitory, doomed, and distorting—that the agreement sought in most assessments is artificial and coerced. That in requiring readers to check their personal biases at the door, we are asking them to, effectively, cease reading. As Seneca wrote two millennia ago: "There is nothing particularly surprising about this way which everyone has of deriving material for their own individual interests from identical subject matter. In one and the same meadow the cow looks for grass, the dog for the hare, and the stork for the lizard" (Seneca, Letter 108).

In this book, Maja Wilson extends the great and uncompromising argument that she started in *Rethinking Rubrics* (2006): that writing teachers and programs have accommodated to assessment practices that were never created to actually serve student growth. Rubrics, grades, and scales are not neutral tools—they retain an intentionality and history. They function to sort, to distribute social goods, to rank and place. Let's take one of the most famous (or infamous) scales, Henry Goddard's delineation of degrees of mental retardation (based on IQ tests)—in ascending order *idiot, imbecile,* and *moron*—a classification that was used into the 1970s (see below). This classification system informed eugenics and forced sterilization efforts, including a famous Supreme Court decision by Oliver Wendell Holmes.

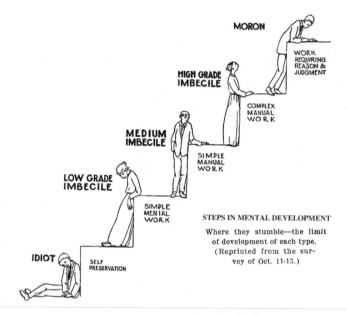

MORON

WORK
REQUIRING
REASON &
JUDGMENT

HIGH GRADE
IMBECILE

COMPLEX
MANUAL
WORK

MEDIUM
IMBECILE

SIMPLE
MANUAL
WORK

LOW GRADE
IMBECILE

SIMPLE
MENTAL
WORK

STEPS IN MENTAL DEVELOPMENT

Where they stumble—the limit
of development of each type.
(Reprinted from the sur-
vey of Oct. 11-13.)

IDIOT

SELF
PRESERVATION

The Binet-Simon Measuring Scale for Intelligence.

Not surprisingly, such scales work to the disadvantage of particularly groups, for example Italian immigrants who would struggle with the English on the IQ tests (the same thing occurred on the infamous tests of U.S. soldiers at the time of World War I). As Milan Kundera once wrote about hierarchies:

> *The very beginning of Genesis tells us that God created*
> *man in order to give him dominion over fish and fowl*
> *and all creatures. Of course, Genesis was written by a man,*
> *not a horse.*

Similarly, Plato placed philosophers at the apex of his republic (and teachers near the bottom).

It may seem a stretch to try to connect eugenics and grading rubrics—but both raise the question: who is assessment serving, the student or the sorting (and labeling) function of the institution? For years I would labor at the end of a semester with assigning grades and wonder, who am I doing this *for*? I could feel the comments I wrote distorted by my need to justify the grade. Although the distinction between formative (for learning) and summative assessment (for final evaluation) is a regular part of the educational lexicon, Wilson argues that formative assessment is often summative-lite—using the same techniques and tools, designed not for learning but for ranking.

As Wilson lays out her elegant argument, she challenges three central premises of scales:

1. that we can predetermine a spectrum (like the prismatic breakdown of light) from bad to good with descriptions of intermediate stages (like the retardation scale)

2. that we can objectively place the student's writing along this scale

3. and that by knowing ones raating on a scale will improve lerning and lead to growth.

I will leave the full argument to her, but in nutshell, all of these premises founder on the fact of novelty. It is an amazing fact of language that even a pedestrian sentence like the one I am now writing has never been written before (nothing came close in a Google search). You are the first to read it. It follows that to respond requires some openness to novelty—and the more a response is predetermined, the less likely it is to be responsive to the creativity of language use. Fitting writing into a predetermined slot is a shortcut that is often called "anchoring"—making a quick categorization based on a few salient features (also a feature of stereotyping). It is a classic problem in diagnosis, particularly under time pressure.

In many rubrics and scales, response is dispensed with entirely, in favor of a delineation of features. Does the writing have a thesis? Check. Does it have evidence? Check. A conclusion? Check. The more we move in this direction, the more viable machine scoring is—and in fact, we have turned human raters into feature-seeking machines, as they "assess" a piece of writing in a matter of seconds. Rubrics regularly fail to offer help to a writer because they focus on what writing has (features) not what writing does (effect). To focus on features may bring about the semblance of objectivity but at the expense of inauthenticity.

Wilson argues that to truly assess writing we need stories, or rather the stories are the assessment. We need multiple stories—of how the piece was written, of where it fits into the writer's development, of the experience of the teacher reading it. It means being open to the uniqueness of the moment—what we are reading has never been written before. Even if we have seen writing on this topic, it is usually a first-time effort by the writer. Whatever its position on a rating scale, it may be a breakthrough for the writer. And the only way we can usefully assess is to tell stories and listen to stories. To create what Peter Elbow has called "movies of our mind": "This is what happened to me as I read this." And movies of the writing: "This is how I came to write this." And movies of our writing history: "This is how this relates to other things I have written."

I suspect that some will find Wilson's position too subjective—in fact, practices in assessment are built on a fear of subjectivity. If we can't locate and judge clear traits or features, the entire enterprise will collapse into idiosyncrasy. We will lose the transparency and objectivity that scales can provide.

This fear is unfounded—otherwise we would never have editors. Or agreement. To tell a story of a reading, to give a movie of the mind, is to show the student *how norms are employed* in the act of reading, how they engage the intentions of the writer. To show where we are engaged, amused, persuaded, lost. A real reader does not fragment the act of assessment into predetermined traits or features: she is alert to the promise of a piece of writing (what it is trying to do), to the stage of the draft, and to the place of the writing in the development of the writer. She draws on a range of norms, values, and observations and asks: what information can help the writer grow?

Subjectivity is a fact of reading, and the fact that no two readers respond the same way is a virtue, not a problem. Each reader approaches a text with a different set of prior experiences, and may prioritize norms in a different way—for example, I am far more tolerant of some disorganization than a lot of other readers (just look at my office). Yet I value (and need) readers less tolerant than I am. It follows that there is a range of useful readings, and this difference can give the writer a sense of how a wider readership might experience her words. The more stories, the better.

There is a dramatic moment in the first act of Wagner's opera, *Die Meistersinger*, when aspiring singer Walther wants to join the guild of singers and has to perform a song he has composed—to be judged by the marker of the guild. Walther's free-form song, inspired by the natural world, violates all the rules of the guild (a sort of strict rubric) and the marker fills a board with symbols of his deviations. Walther is stopped before finishing. Only the shoemaker Sachs is able to respond and sings this defense:

> *The knight's song and melody*
> *I found new, but not confused;*
> *if he left our paths*
> *he at least strode firmly and surely.*
> *If you wish to measure according to rules*
> *something which does not agree with your rules,*
> *forget your own ways,*
> *and first seek its rules!*

This is the challenge Maja Wilson poses for us—to be responsive, open to novelty. And to proclaim our loyalty to the learner and not be simply agents of the institutional sorting machine.

Introduction: Beyond *Rethinking Rubrics*

i loved everything about teaching writing at Ludington High School in Michigan—except for the thirty-minute lunches, the final exam policy, and the rubrics. I could scarf a peanut butter sandwich in four minutes flat and write a creatively subversive exam if I needed to, but rubrics irritated me to no end.

I first noticed a problem with the rubric's ability to capture writing quality when Ed wrote an elegant and insightful one-sentence answer. Since he didn't restate the question or provide three sentences of support, his answer should have failed the Constructed Response Rubric I was using to score it. I'd actually helped to create this schoolwide rubric and had led a faculty inservice on how to use it several months earlier.

I had two choices: apply the rubric faithfully and ignore Ed's clever command of the material, or admit that I'd been backed into a corner of my own making. It took me all of three seconds to decide (I fudged the rubric), but the moment stuck with me and set the stage for further inquiry into the promises and pitfalls of rubrics.

Ed's answer reminded me that any evaluation tool is doomed if it fails to accommodate the human need to resist arbitrary rules. Perhaps if I simply got rid of those silly length requirements! Over the course of several years, I tried the 6 Trait^R and the 6+1 Trait^R Rubrics. I rewrote existing rubrics and created my own. I played with analytic and holistic designs. I even invited students to make rubrics with me. But through every one of these informal trials, I ran smack into the same problems, which I eventually articulated in *Rethinking Rubrics in Writing Assessment* (Wilson 2006).

Published while I was a high school teacher, *Rethinking Rubrics* was largely a critique. I won't shy away from critique in *Reimagining Writing Assessment: From Scales to Stories*. But I'll move beyond critique, too. I'll build a case: we should replace the scales embedded in rubrics with new tools. One possible set of new tools? Stories and an array of interpretive lenses designed to observe and describe growth.

In this introduction, I'll summarize my critique of rubrics (and throw in some new thinking, too). This will provide background for readers unfamiliar with *Rethinking Rubrics* and set a direction for the alternative tools I'll describe later in this book. Ultimately, these tools can be judged by how they respond to the critique that motivated them.

Rubrics Oversimplify a Complex Process and Overcomplexify Everything in the Process

When I began investigating my dissatisfaction with rubrics, the first thing I noticed was that rubrics reduce an essay to the sum of its parts. In some rubrics, this literally means the parts of the essay: introduction, body, and conclusion. These parts are often further fractured: the introduction into lead and thesis; the body paragraphs into topic sentences, examples, and transitions; and the conclusion into a restatement of the thesis and clincher statement. After being scored separately, these subparts are then added back up to form a global score.

Most rubrics, however, don't break the essay into literal parts. Instead, they break quality into abstract parts—factors, traits, or criteria such as organization and word choice. These are then plugged into a simple formula designed to predict writing quality. The 6+1 Trait[R] Rubric, for example, can be rewritten as this formula:

Ideas + Organization + Voice + Word Choice
+ Sentence Fluency + Conventions + Presentation
= The Quality of the Writing

Of course, if the formula were really this simple, the 6+1 Trait[R] would be two lines long. But at fourteen pages, I found this rubric bulkier than any essay I was evaluating. Why is a tool that attempts to *simplify* writing assessment so long? Despite its gesture toward straightforward mathematical simplicity, the rubric attempts to answer what turns out to be a truly complex philosophical question: how can writing quality be determined? When it can't answer the complexity of that question, the rubric spins out of control.

The first symptom of the question's complexity is the fact that readers regularly disagree about writing quality. This can't be chalked up to the fact that some readers are just "bad." In fact, the field of literary criticism would die a very quick death if disagreement between experts were the exception and not the rule. Even Educational Testing Service (ETS) knows that readers disagree—or, at least, its own researchers discovered it in 1961.

By 1948, the College Board English Composition Test didn't ask students to compose anything, relying instead on "objective-type" test items such as multiple-choice grammar questions (Elliot 2005, 159). The stakes were high—various colleges and universities required the English Composition Test for admission—and teachers protested that a high-stakes test stripped of writing consequently stripped the classroom of writing. In response, the College Board introduced the Interlinear "test" in 1950: a short passage that included awkward sentences and various errors. Students were to write their revisions between the lines—thus, the name of the test (Olsen and Swineford 1953, 1). Because it required students to propose their own revisions rather than asking them to choose between answers, Interlinear was deemed by ETS researchers to evaluate "creative action rather than mere recognition" (Olsen and Swineford 1953, 2).

For many, Interlinear didn't go far enough. Revising someone else's awkward sentence is not the same as imagining, planning, and writing your own composition. In 1960, the College Board committee was told that several member colleges might drop the English Composition test. In response to the "hubbub" (Elliot 2005, 159) that followed this announcement, the committee formulated a recommendation: "Since we are testing a skill, and since the skill is called writing competency, should we not, for the first time . . . use . . . essays written under standard testing conditions and read by people who normally read such essays . . . ?" (Godshalk, cited in Elliot 2005, 159).

ETS followed with several investigations into just such an essay test. The central question: could readers agree on scores? To answer this, Paul Diederich, John French, and Sydell Carlton (1961) asked fifty-three "esteemed readers" to rate over 300 student papers on a 1- to 9-point scale. The results weren't encouraging: not a single paper received less than five different scores, and 94 percent of the papers received seven different ratings.

But this wasn't disinterested research, so these findings were never published under the headlines that would actually describe them: "Esteemed Readers Disagree!" or "Research Confirms: Writing Assessment Incompatible with Standardized Testing!" Sponsored by the largest standardized testing company in the world, the researchers' goal was to make the evaluation of essays compatible with standardized testing. So instead of being declared the *finding* of the study, reader disagreement was defined from the beginning as a *problem* for the study to solve.

To solve this so-called problem, Diederich and his colleagues would need to manufacture agreement. Toward this end, they employed educational measurement's most powerful tools: fragmentation and reductionism. First, they organized all the comments made on the 300+ student papers into fifty-five categories. Then they reduced these categories to five factors of writing quality—ideas, form, flavor, mechanics, and wording. These factors are the basis for most scoring guides or rubrics today.

No matter the wording of the factors, they all "work" in the same way, by narrowing readers' focus. To understand how a narrowed focus manufactures agreement, just remember that consistent ratings are easy enough if you ask readers to count words and assign ratings based on, say, length. This may seem a ridiculously extreme example, until you realize that ETS' own computer essay grading system (Criterion) actually employs length as a measure of quality. But factors such as ideas or organization are more open to interpretation for human readers than a computer program's calculations of length, so ETS developed a reader calibration procedure to further standardize readers' ratings. This calibration procedure dismisses readers whose ratings don't consistently agree. Through calibrating readers to the rubric or scoring guide, ETS could achieve sufficient interrater reliability for the purposes of standardized testing.

Still, these attempts evaded the complex question of how we determine or experience the quality of the writing. *No worries!* The rubric attempts to soothe us. *You needn't determine the quality of the essay!*

You just have to figure out the quality of the essay's organization, ideas, style, sentence fluency, and conventions! At which point, we inevitably find ourselves asking, "Well, how do I evaluate the quality of an essay's voice?" This, too, is a philosophically charged and complicated question. Following the logic that smaller things are easier to evaluate than bigger things, the rubric passes the buck again, breaking voice into increasingly smaller parts. For example, consider how the 6+1 Trait[R] Rubric breaks down the assessment for the trait of voice into five additional modifying traits:

> Engagement with Reader + Individual Expression
> + Tone + Commitment + Fit with
> Audience/Purpose

Not surprisingly, this second evasion only works momentarily, as the question resurfaces: "OK, but how do I evaluate a modifying trait like individual expression?" Once again, the rubric responds the only way it knows how—by further avoidance and reduction. This time, each modifying trait is broken into six different descriptors aligned to a 6-point scale.

Let's pause for some math of our own. With 43 separate categories of writing quality each divided into 6 performance descriptors in the 6+1 Trait[R] Rubric, we're talking about 258 possible evaluations. From these 258 descriptors, we are supposed to select 36, which are then roughly added and averaged into 7 separate trait scores, which we then add and average into a single score representing global writing quality. By refusing to engage the complexity of the question about how readers evaluate writing, the rubric becomes evasive and ultimately unwieldy. Which is why the 6+1 Trait[R] Rubric is 13 + 1 pages long.

The more specific a rubric becomes in its attempt to reduce and pin down the evaluation, the more assumptions we have to accept (or ignore) to use it. The 6+1 Trait[R] Rubric assumes that these traits are the seven that matter most for writing quality. But what about traits not included, such as humor or originality? There's also the question of whether each category is significantly related to the trait it modifies. Consider the subtrait of individual expression, which modifies the trait of voice. Is voice always a function of individual expression?

I recently read *Authoring*, a book with a powerful, elegant, and uncompromising voice. However, this voice can hardly be the product of individual expression. Instead, it is the product of collaboration, because the book is coauthored by Richard Haswell and Janis Haswell (2010).

Finally, there's the question of whether the performance indicators for each subtrait accurately represent a range of quality. Consider the lowest descriptor for individual expression: "Reveals virtually nothing specific about the author." We don't need to be familiar with the authorial intention debate in literary studies to question the idea that individual expression requires authors to reveal specific personal details. Sometimes, sure. In fact, I conjured up personal details from my high school teaching experience (including my ability to quickly eat a peanut butter sandwich and my dilemma with Ed's one-sentence answer) on the first page of this book in order to ally myself with teacher-readers. However, I also considered opening the book with an analogy, describing a medical diagnosis tool acknowledged to have caused more harm than good for patients with back pain: MRIs. I have no experience with back pain or MRIs, so this opening would have revealed nothing specific about me. But this impersonal rhetorical choice would not, I hope, have signaled a lack of individual expression or voice.

Questioning any one of these assumptions threatened to derail me every time I tried to use this rubric. But I have nothing in particular against the 6+1 Trait^R Rubric. I have found every rubric I have ever tried to use just as frustrating as this one, even those I have created. As I wrote *Rethinking Rubrics*, I realized that the real problem wasn't the wording or even the focus of the traits, which meant that never-ending revisions of the criteria or descriptors wasn't the solution. My real problem was with two assumptions at the heart of all rubrics.

The rubric's first assumption is that the traits of writing interact with each other in predictable ways to create quality (Trait 1 + Trait 2 . . . = Writing Quality). To question this assumption, I borrowed a scientific explanation for the interaction of factors within systems. In deterministic systems, a limited number of factors interact in predictable ways. Therefore, simple formulas work perfectly well for describing and predicting outcomes. For example, the game of billiards is a simple system, so if you want to know where a billiard ball will go when hit with a certain amount of force in a certain direction, you simply measure the pertinent factors, plug these measurements into the pertinent formula, and voilà! You can know with certainty where the ball will go.

The rubric treats texts as deterministic systems. Figure out the factors of quality (Ideas + Word Choice . . .), measure them, add them up, and you can know with certainty how good the text is. However, a text didn't seem like a deterministic system to me, and using deterministic formulas to predict outcomes for complex systems simply doesn't work. First, you can't identify all the factors involved. Furthermore, the factors are so subtle that no instruments can accurately measure them. In addition, the factors are so dynamic that you can't measure them often enough (even if you had the instruments to do so). To fatally confound all predictive efforts, the factors in complex systems are chaotic—they don't interact in predictable ways. It's why we're no good at predicting long-term global weather.

The human beings who read texts introduce complexity and chaos into the system. After all, texts aren't written to be autonomous objects. They are written *to be read*, to create experiences within readers. So they cannot be evaluated outside these experiences—one reader at a time. This seems a stupidly obvious point until you remember that computer programs are being used today to evaluate writing. Even marketers don't dare claim these programs can "read." So it's a point worth asserting and defending: texts exist to be read and cannot be evaluated outside the act of reading. And reading, unlike billiards, is a marvelously complex process.

To understand the complexity of reading within a single reader (never mind between two different readers!), consider a text you read years ago and revisited recently. Perhaps you were appalled to find that your favorite book when you were thirteen now strikes you as whiny. Or, that a poem you dragged yourself through in eleventh-grade English class now paints your entire life with startling clarity. It simply isn't fair to resolve this disjunction by denigrating your younger self's judgment. If you do, you'll have to acknowledge that a similar shift in judgment might happen in the future, rendering *today's* judgment just as null as your thirteen-year-old self's. Either you must prophylactically disparage every textual evaluation you ever make, or you must acknowledge that reading, and therefore writing evaluation, is complex: subjective, shifting, anything but predictable.

Your subjectivity isn't a problem to be solved. You come to each text a different reader each time, bringing your experiences and purposes in a particular moment to bear on each of your readings. This isn't just the best you can muster; it's the only way to make meaning from what you read. And it's not just the way it works because of your flawed human nature or your lack of objective criteria that experts supposedly possess. Your subjectivity is actually the way reading is *supposed* to work. Texts exist to do real work in real readers who bring themselves to each reading. Why else would anyone read? Why else would anyone write?

But we're not just talking about one complex system; beyond the reader, there's the text—itself the product of a human writer's interaction with language and the rhetorical context. Throw all these complex systems into the petri dish, let them react, and watch what grows. It's simply wishful thinking to imagine any rubric can accurately predict the outcome. Therefore, it really doesn't matter if a rubric gets all the traits and their performance descriptors right. And it doesn't matter who writes it—ETS, your English department, you, or your students. Trying to use a determinist formula like a rubric to predict the outcome of this complex and chaotic interaction is a recipe for bad science—ill fated at best and perverse at worse. And if a rubric can't accurately predict quality when used by an evaluator, it surely won't inspire quality when consulted beforehand by a writer. That's why Ed's insightful sentence could only be written because he ignored my rubric (and I knew Ed well enough to know that *defied* may have been a more accurate term than *ignored*).

Beyond questioning the ways that textual traits interact to constitute quality, I questioned whether readers actually value textual traits directly—a key assumption of all rubrics. However, I think that readers value their *experience* of textual traits. Although not idiosyncratic, these experiences are highly personal. This slight shift in emphasis—from textual traits to the reader's experience of the trait—explains the prevalence of reader disagreement and thereby changes everything about writing assessment.

If Not Rubrics, Then What Instead?

In *Rethinking Rubrics*, I didn't pretend to solve the problem of how to evaluate writing without rubrics. With their pitfalls just barely acknowledged, I thought it too early to propose "The Assessment Alternative." Although some readers faulted me for this, I am confident that more problems have been created by hasty solutions than have ever been solved. As composition scholar Chris Anson puts it,

> *More often than not . . . the field of composition has erred when it has too hastily trusted and laid claim to certainty. . . . Instead of providing solutions, the urge for certainty has often created new problems by encouraging simpleminded mechanical procedures for teaching or learning highly complex skills and processes. (1989, 2)*

Instead, I contributed what I considered to be a prerequisite for solutions: principles that could be used to create promising alternatives.

In *Rethinking Rubrics*, I proposed that writing assessment should:

- **Honor rhetorical purpose and effect.** Assessment should honor the way that words affect a reader's mind, and encourage writers to understand that writing is assessed by readers who bring different understandings and experiences to their readings and assessment.

- **Be responsive and encourage new insights.** Assessment should allow us to identify our values in reaction to a specific piece of writing. Therefore, we must teach readers (including ourselves!) to pay attention to what they think and feel as they read and to explain their reactions in helpful ways to authors—a *metacognitive reading.*

- **Understand disagreement by exploring a reader's context and the author's purpose.** If we encourage readers to pay attention to their reactions to writing, we open the door to *disagreement*. Dealing with disagreements means exploring a reader's *position* or *context*: what experiences, background, or assumptions lead a reader to a particular assessment?

- **Encourage readers to articulate their positions.** In this way, we shift the responsibility of transparency from the clear external standards of rubrics to the internal standards, assumptions, and experiences that readers bring to their readings and assessments.

- **Teach student authors how to extract clarity from disagreement through careful study of readers' context and their own purposes.** After studying dissent and where it comes from, the author is in a better position to understand and articulate how these views fit or do not fit into the author's intent. (2006, 64–65)

You'll notice that all of these principles include the word *reader*. That's because I first noticed how much I disliked rubrics when I noticed how they changed my reading of student work. While grounded in experiences and values I outlined in *Rethinking Rubrics*, my work in this book represents a slight shift in focus. In *Reimagining Writing Assessment*, I attempt to put a writer's experience and needs consciously at the center of what writing assessment should be.

As it turns out, the experiences and needs of writers is a radical starting point for writing assessment theory and practice. Most assessment theory and practice has been guided by institutional concerns and a very coherent vision for social, economic, and educational stratification. In fact, assessment is key to the realization of this vision because it functions as the mechanism for determining how we allocate our collective resources and opportunities. We'd be wise to consider what this vision is, where and why it began in the first place, and where it leads. Otherwise, we run the risk of unwittingly participating in a system that violates our values.

The alternative assessment practices I will describe in this book will not neatly replace the rubric and appease the systems of accountability that currently shape assessment. That's because they serve different interests than those served by the accountability movement. In the ten years since *Rethinking Rubrics* was published, I've researched the ideas and historical figures that have shaped this societal vision and limited our conception of what assessment can be. I'll relate some of that story to help explain why true alternatives are so doggedly difficult to create and sustain—and why it is so critically important that we do so.

Because my vision of writing assessment is centered in the moment that a teacher and a student are brought together by the authoring of a text, my proposal does not directly address assessment used by testing companies or state agencies for the purposes of accountability. That's another book. This book is for teachers who want to honor their students' experiences as writers and readers—and their own. Of course, if we take this moment between teacher and student and text seriously, writing assessment as it's constructed by testing companies and the accountability movement will have to change, as well. I don't care who is using the assessment and what the assessment is being used for: if the SAT or the state test or the program assessment makes it more difficult for teachers to help students grow as writers in their own classrooms, then it needs to change.

Of course, the SAT and the district's common assessment won't change tomorrow just because I've declared it needs to. But these powerful institutional assessments have the effect of making those who matter most in the assessment equation—teachers and students—less clear about what they know. The less clear we are, the more likely we'll be to accept something that violates our knowledge and beliefs. A commitment to clarity is, in itself, an important act of resistance and change.

Despite significant systematic obstacles to enacting some of the practices I'll describe in this book, I maintain that there are still spaces left in education—in our relationships with the students in our care, in our conversations with colleagues and parents, and in our political participations—for us to resist, to protest, and even to reimagine assessment and our own profession. I believe that we have a personal, professional, and civic responsibility to do so.

Resist, protest, reimagine. These may not be words you wanted to think about at the beginning of a book about assessment. Part of me wants to assure you not to worry. *You're just reading a book after all! You don't have to* do *anything. What's the worst that can happen?* But if you're an English teacher, you know full well that reading and writing can be subversive and even dangerous acts, requiring courage. In this book, I very strongly suggest that our assessments cannot simultaneously serve the writers in our classrooms and the demands of accountability as it is currently constructed. That's not an easy message to face.

However, I suspect that a good many teachers know this on some level already. Furthermore, I suspect that this knowledge causes a great deal of professional despair. I have felt this acutely, and the only antidote I have ever found is to articulate, as clearly as I am able, the causes and consequences of this despair. Only then can I imagine and pursue a course of action that allows my students to experience for themselves the profound joy and challenge that the written word has provided me. I know of no other way to teach.

Feedback *Is* the Answer!

"But Wait, What Do **You** *Mean by Feedback?"*

"What's your greatest weakness?" The question is every job candidate's worst nightmare. Offer a fault that is really an asset ("I just care too much!"), and you risk looking disingenuous. Answer honestly, and you might slip in the rankings if other candidates don't fess up to a real flaw. To prepare for my first interview for a high school English teaching position, I'd tucked a carefully crafted strength-in-disguise up my sleeve. When the question was actually posed, however, I couldn't bring myself to pull it out.

Instead, I told the truth: I wasn't sure it was my *greatest* weakness, but I struggled greatly with grading. It wasn't something I'd been expected to do very often in my three years of teaching Adult Basic Education and Secondary Alternative Education. More importantly,

I worried that grades discouraged the very students who needed the most encouragement. Many of my adult students had dropped out of high school precisely because their grades had convinced them that they couldn't learn. I hadn't yet read Alfie Kohn's critique of grades or Edward Deci and Richard Ryan's research on how extrinsic motivators undermine performance, interest, and creativity (Kohn 1993; Ryan and Deci 1985, 2000). I just knew from experience that grades too often got in the way of the good stuff. Furthermore, although I enjoyed the intellectual challenge of reading and responding to students' writing, grading bored me. So I avoided it as often as I could.

My honesty didn't work against me, and I taught happily in that district for the next seven years. But I never resolved my struggle with grading. If anything, it got worse. And because I equated assessment with grading, it probably isn't surprising that I took a rather dim view of assessment. Still, I didn't want to be seen as someone who dismissed assessment entirely. How could I reimagine assessment? When I wrote *Rethinking Rubrics* (2006), I knew I wanted to unhinge assessment from grades. But what would that look like?

Could Feedback Replace Rubrics?

I considered response to student writers one of my most sacred professional duties. So for several years, I insisted that response and feedback could salvage assessment—that it *was* assessment. After all, my responses to writers were rooted in my assessment of what they needed as writers and my experience of their texts. I believed that the format of conversation (whether spoken or written) could better accommodate the speculative and shifting nature of assessment—and interactions with the writer—that I valued.

So I started paying attention to anything in the assessment literature that mentioned feedback. When Ruth Culham published a book about constructive feedback in 2006, I purchased it immediately. I'd already critiqued Culham's vision of rubric-driven writing assessment. However, I'd come to understand that rubrics were designed to generate scores (see *Rethinking Rubrics* and the introduction to this book). I assumed that an individual reader's response to an individual writer wouldn't have much to do with grades, so I thought that Culham and I might find common ground on feedback.

As it turns out, the push for standardization inherent in grades and rubrics had exerted a similarly standardizing influence on Culham's conception of feedback. In *100 Trait-Specific Comments: A Quick Guide for Giving Constructive Feedback on Student Writing*, Culham offers 100 "just-right" responses to students' essays. Organized by conveniently color-coded tabs, each comment corresponds to a trait and a score and can simply be copied onto students' papers. Scoring and response, in one fell swoop! I found the results hilariously perverse. For example, this comment appears under the aqua-colored tab for voice: "This piece sounds like you. It really sings out with your voice!" (2006, 13)

When I shared Culham's book with students in my twelfth-grade research writing class, they immediately appreciated the ironies. How could a teacher parrot someone else's voice to praise the uniqueness of a student's voice? And why should a student who had composed her own essay settle for a response that her teacher had plagiarized? We agreed that the last section, Personal Comments, did nothing to undo the impersonal vision of feedback presented in the book:

> *You will develop your own favorite comments to use on students' papers as you practice with the ones in this guide. Use these pages to record these comments so you have them for future reference. (2006, 22)*

The idea that I might forget and thus wish to record my own favorite comments for future reference made me chuckle. But the underlying assumptions were more troubling than amusing. In this formulation of feedback, comments do not arise in the context of a true exchange. Rather, they are discrete items to be developed— commodities to be produced, reproduced, and, in the case of Culham's comments, *sold*.

It is true that we sometimes find ourselves making the same comments over and over on students' papers. But when I notice myself becoming a skipping human record, I'm not tempted to further standardize the process. Instead, the repetition alerts me that something may be wrong. In my view of feedback, every response constitutes an interaction between two human beings. At their best, my responses express my experience of reading a particular text and my understanding of the student's writing process and development. If nothing else, Culham's standardized feedback was helping me articulate what I meant (and didn't mean) by feedback.

Hitting Those Learning Targets and Other Acts of Violence in Assessment

As it turns out, feedback was enjoying a groundswell of support in the mainstream discourse about formative assessment. The rhetoric sounded good: feedback was heralded as a way to put growth ahead of grading, ranking, and sorting. However, the more I examined it, the more I realized that this version of feedback couldn't do what I wanted feedback to do; it didn't accommodate readers' experiences and it wasn't responsive to writers' intentions. In addition, I began to see a violent underside to the ways in which feedback was being conceptualized and used in this discourse.

I first clued into my differences with mainstream proponents of formative assessment when I read Rick Stiggins' call for assessments that "promote hope" (2005, 325). In his oft-cited article, "From Formative Assessment to Assessment FOR Learning: A Path to Success...", Stiggins explains,

> *[In assessment FOR teaching and learning] the teacher provides learners with continuous access to descriptive feedback which consists not merely of grades or scores but also of focused guidance specific to the learning target. (2005, 328)*

Descriptive feedback. I briefly thought that Stiggins and I might be singing the same tune. But something about the word *target* at the end of the sentence made me pause. Was *target* simply a synonym for *purposes* or *intentions*, both words I'd be much more likely to use? Or did semantic differences indicate more fundamental philosophical divergences?

Two administrators helped me to understand how learning targets are used in the mainstream view of formative assessment—and why they make me uneasy. The first administrator appeared in a YouTube video titled, "Setting Measures of Academic Progress." In it, the principal stands in a second-grade classroom next to a chart of test scores titled, "It's About Growth." As the teacher stands silently nearby, the principal calls out, "Data is . . ." and gestures for the second graders to fill in the blank, which they do in perfect singsong rhythm: "Data is . . . *fabulous.*" Then, she announces, "We're going to talk about your growth. We're going to go over where you were, and what the target was, and then, did you meet it?"

The principal points to the first cell on the chart. "So, in the fall, in math, you had an average RIT score of . . ." She lets students call out the answer, "One hundred seventy-six! OK, and we set a goal for you, didn't we? And how many RIT points were you hoping to gain in this class?" At the correct answer, she nods, repeating, "Ten points."

Then, the moment they've all been waiting for. The principal grasps the sticky note that covers the results and pauses, teasing a bit, "Thumbs up or thumbs down, did you make it?" The students gasp in anticipation while the principal slowly pulls back the note. When the score is revealed—*186!*—the class erupts in squeals and enthusiastic applause. After repeating the same process for reading and language usage and one final round of "Data is *fabulous*!," the principal announces, "[Your teacher] and I got together and we already set your spring targets. Maybe we can show you those today" ("Setting Measures of Academic Progress Goals" 2010).

Just as Stiggins would advocate, the administrator is sharing feedback about students' growth in relation to learning targets, and she's doing so in a way that promotes hope (or, at least, *enthusiasm*). But the devil is in the details. In this scene, *targets* are goals that consist of test-generated data points, and *growth* is the difference between one test score and another. It's all very rational, all very convenient. But the convenience comes at the cost of meaning. Although everyone cheers passionately, no one knows what growing 8 points in reading means. Reducing growth to a numerical change in test scores makes a joke of the complex work of learning and the nature of knowledge and skills.

It inflicts on children the very same misguided fixation with test scores that uninformed policy makers have been peddling for decades.

Several years later, a high school administrator animated learning targets, alerting me to the violent overtones. I was at a workshop in Maine on proficiency-based education (PBE), a framework that replaces traditional grades with a collection of learning targets and rubrics for each course. The principal stood to describe how PBE had influenced assessment at his school, slamming his fist into his palm every time he said the word *hit*: "When you're measuring learning targets, you might *hit* it, but you're going to have to go back and re-*hit* it. So it's multiple *hits*, really."

The metaphor was clearly alive for this principal, as he paired *target* with the verb *hit* and gave it life through gesture. I'd never been fond of the word *standards*, but at least there was nothing violent about it. *Hitting a learning target*, on the other hand, explicitly conjured up a bulls-eye and a weapon. Never mind that there are children nearby. I emailed the scene to a colleague, who replied simply, "Pedagogy of the abused."

Of course, there is no hint of violence in the actual definition of a learning target, described by Connie Moss, Susan Brookhart, and Beverly Long as the "precise 'chunk' of the content students are to master" (2011, 66), written in student-friendly language. But the principal isn't alone in emphasizing the implied hostility. Moss, Brookhart, and Long open their article with the story of young Joey, who walks into school one morning wearing a tie-dye T-shirt. Another student notices the colorful concentric circles and calls out, "'Look, Joey, you're wearing a learning target!'" (2011, 66). In a video, students create and hang their own red and white construction paper targets. Each performance level has a kid-friendly and target-appropriate name. The outer circle, the teacher reports with glee, is labeled "Ouch!"

I'm fairly certain that these educators do not interact violently with children. But the violence in the metaphor reflects the violence embedded in our society's use of assessment: when we look more closely, we see that learning targets, assessments, and feedback are important gears in a powerful societal tracking system that cannot, by virtue of its design, lead to better outcomes for more people. That's because this system was designed to create and maintain hierarchies. When feedback and assessment are built around fixed learning targets, they easily serve a controlled, bureaucratic version of education that protects the unequal distribution of resources. Individual educators don't need to share these aims—or even be aware of them—to participate in them.

Mapping the Mixed Metaphors: Targets, Global Positioning Systems, and Fitbits

To understand how assessment, learning targets, and feedback serve less egalitarian ends—despite the rhetoric about "promoting hope" (Stiggins 2005, 325)—we'll examine another popular metaphor in this discourse: assessment as Global Positioning System, or GPS (Stiggins and Chapuis 2012, 12; Moss, Brookhart, and Long 2011, 66). Here's how the metaphor works. The student is a traveler who must navigate the map of learning. Her destination? Educational achievement and a good life. To help her get there, the GPS calculates her route—a sequence of learning targets that stretches from her current location to her intended destination. First, the GPS must determine exactly where the student is currently located. That's formative assessment's job; it locates the student in relation to the learning target. Next, the GPS *feeds* this location *back* to the traveler and tells her where to go next. On the GPS map, that's the little dot that moves when you move. In a classroom, it's the continuous stream of feedback consisting of "focused guidance specific to the learning target" (Stiggins 2005, 328) provided by the teacher or standardized assessment. Once you define feedback as information about the student's distance from a learning target, it's easy to reduce feedback to assessment's version of binary code: test data or the standardized "descriptors" on a rubric's performance levels. This explains how something like Culham's color-coded comments or the principal's celebration of test data can be taken seriously as feedback.

But we're not done with the metaphors. The GPS provides direction, but what about the student's motivation to keep moving along the path of learning targets? Enter the feedback Fitbit. A Fitbit is a tracking and motivational device that counts every step you take and vibrates when you've met your goals. I'm not making this up: Kathy Dyer explains how feedback in a classroom is like a Fitbit that keeps students going in an entry for the Formative Assessment section of Northwest Education Association's education blog:

> If it is 9 PM at night and my tracker tells me I am 237 steps short of my goal, guess what I do before I go to bed? I walk 237 steps . . . when we help students track their progress through visually vibrant displays of their data, they get a quick read on where they are in their learning . . . Some of these fitness trackers provide feedback along with the data. Some allow you to earn badges. For some of us, these provide feelings of accomplishment . . . Feedback allows students to get a picture of where they are in relation to the goal and reflect on what they've learned. I have colleagues who smile big when their tracker vibrates and the lights flash. The feeling of accomplishment is important, just as it is for our students. (2015)

In this formulation, learning to write is akin to taking 237 more steps before bedtime or turning left where the nice British lady says to turn. Thus, feedback is both trivialized and standardized.

How Learning Fitbits Can Undermine Motivation

There's something obsessive about all the feedback in the GPS and Fitbit metaphors. I remember the only horseback riding lesson I ever took from my mother. Before I'd been in the saddle ten minutes, I was spewing constant commentary on how I thought I was doing and asking endless anxious questions about how my performance compared to the ideal. In other words, I wanted continuous feedback. Exasperated, my mother told me to close my eyes. She would lead the horse, and I was to concentrate on what it *felt* like to ride. No talking, no feedback. I learned more in that silence than at any other point during the lesson.

You'll never hear me argue that teachers shouldn't ever give feedback. But feedback isn't inherently good—something that every child, employee, student, friend, and spouse or partner is likely to have intuited at some point or another. Sometimes, feedback is helpful from one person and annoying or even damaging from another. Sometimes, feedback distracts. Sometimes, feedback paralyzes. Sometimes, feedback destroys the relationship. And sometimes, feedback makes us dependent on the feedback and not on our own motivations.

Feeding kids a constant stream of assessment data can actually undermine their learning, motivation, interest, and achievement. As those who have struggled with perfectionism or self-consciousness can attest, sometimes you need to ignore everyone's judgment (including your own) and, well, *just do it*. My mother knew this during my riding lesson. Composition scholar Peter Elbow knew it when he wrote, "Closing My Eyes as I Speak: An Argument for Ignoring Audience" (1987). And psychological researchers know it from scores of studies they've conducted and synthesized on motivation and a performance or achievement focus versus a learning focus (Butler 1987; Dweck 1999, 2006; Ryan and Deci 1985, 2000; Brophy 2005; Darnon 2008).

According to Deci and Ryan (2000), intrinsic motivation is the urge to do something because it's experienced as inherently worth doing, and extrinsic motivation is the urge to do something because it "leads to a separable outcome" (55). When teachers give students "continuous" feedback on how well they've hit or missed learning targets (no matter if the students have participated in setting the targets), we are requiring students to focus, almost obsessively, on their performance—on extrinsic motivators. Doing so, the research suggests, makes students more likely to write or read not because *this is interesting* but because *I need to perform better at this*. The result? Performance, creativity, and interest decrease. Whether written as "Needs improvement" or "Ouch," performance levels function no differently than grades in undermining intrinsic motivation.

The Fitbit vibrations that cause Kathy Dyer's colleagues to smile warmly may be just fine for counting your steps. After all, the research indicates that rewards *do* work as motivators for the simplest of mechanical skills. But once rudimentary cognitive skill is involved (for activities such as, um . . . learning to read and write), rewards kill both interest and performance (Pink 2009). When feedback is constructed as praise for meeting learning targets, it is based on a discredited twentieth-century theory of motivation, even though twenty-first-century analogies are invoked to support it.

Educational Chutes and Ladders: Assessment's Role in the Game of Inequality

And that's just the psychological problem with these metaphors. The structural problem is more troubling still. The implication is that any learner can succeed if educators identify the right targets, administer the right assessments, and give the right feedback. *Just get the latest mapping technology, and use it!* However, when we peel back the top layer of this metaphoric map of learning, we see something that looks less like a navigational tool and more like a Chutes and Ladders game. By design, a competitive game creates more losers than winners. And this is precisely what happens at every level of schooling: assessments determine whether learners slide down to remedial tracks or climb up to exclusive institutions and opportunities that lead to wealth and political influence. Of course, assessments such as the SAT are correlated strongly not with effort or instruction, but with family wealth ("2013 College-Bound Seniors..." [2013]). Thus, those who begin the game ahead not only have a head start, but also a higher chance of landing on a ladder than a chute.

To add insult to injury on one hand and benefit to privilege on the other, this Educational Chutes and Ladders game is rigged in multiple ways. Some children use playing boards that begin with underfunded public schools in poverty-stricken neighborhoods. Winners of this game might climb to community college or second-tier state universities and join the middle class, but most will struggle to eke out a living. Children with access to family and community wealth not only start the game ahead, but play on completely different boards, with the benefit of highly competitive (and expensive) private schools, tutors, test-prep classes, and access to elite institutions. Winners of these game boards become president or senators or tech moguls or lobbyists. From their positions of power, wealth, and influence, these predestined winners continue to write the rules in ways that favor their own children and others who look, act, and think like them.

Every once in a while, the tests pluck a student from the underfunded public school game board and whisk him away to one of the elite private boarding school game boards. Offered as evidence of education's role in class mobility, these exceptions to the rule hide the ways in which the tests were designed to keep players and boards separate—and the ways in which they ensure that there are always a few winners but mostly losers. A few representatives from the lower classes can be tolerated if it keeps the peace by maintaining the illusion of meritocracy.

Portraying these multiple rigged game boards as a single map that anyone can navigate with the right feedback distorts reality and obscures the game's function: to propel a select few to wealth and influence. Helping students score better on the assessments doesn't necessarily create more winners. When more students demonstrate mastery, the cut scores simply increase—a phenomenon that has historically expressed itself in complaints about grade inflation and the drive for higher standards and more rigorous tests. And, of course, elite institutions don't admit more students when more students score better. In fact, they market high rejection rates, selling their exclusivity (Perez-Pena 2014). Decades of socioeconomic data reflect the futility of trying to help individual students succeed without addressing structural inequality: the nation's wealth is being controlled by an increasingly smaller percentage of the population while more and more people live in poverty (Gilson and Perot 2011; Stiglitz 2011).

Formative Assessment's Squandered Promise

Of course, the real culprit here is high-stakes testing, which was designed from the outset to play this gatekeeping function. I'm hardly the first teacher or scholar to cry foul. Teachers of all ages and scholars in numerous fields have protested testing's effects, and resistance has taken multiple forms. Some have refused to administer the tests. Some have opposed the tests' impact on curriculum. Some have refused to teach to the tests. Some have exposed bias in test questions. Some have pushed testing companies to incorporate assessment tools developed for classroom use, such as portfolios. Some have exposed the tests' eugenic origins and uses. Some have argued to lessen the frequency and stakes of the tests.

The formative assessment movement represents another form of resistance—or, at least, the potential for it. The promise goes like this: although summative assessment might be designed by educational measurement and used by institutions to punish or reward, formative assessment is designed by teachers to help students. Designed for different purposes, it honors different sources of knowledge: a teacher's understanding of the meaning of *that* look on *this* student's face, for instance, or the wisdom required to scrap a well-designed lesson plan because a few students were chanting "Build the wall!" at lunchtime, tensions are high, and *now what?* Educational measurement has no procedures or tools to help teachers observe and interpret the everyday ebb and flow of interaction and relationship in the classroom. This is the realm of formative assessment. It's homegrown, bottom-up, and local. It's artisanal, but not rare: millions of teachers have what it takes.

That's the promise, anyway. The reality too often resembles a Trojan horse, as testing companies use formative assessment to usher the tools and techniques of high-stakes testing into the classroom in new and insidious ways. There's a price to pay for this invasion. *Education Week*'s Special Report landed in my mailbox just yesterday. Inside, an article about digital formative assessments proclaimed, "Schools are expected to spend nearly $1.6 billion this year on classroom assessment tools" (Molnar 2017, 28). That's more money, the author claims, than the $1.3 billion that will be spent on state-mandated tests. Formative assessment is big business.

Often, the companies that design and administer high-stakes standardized tests are the same companies that market and sell these so-called formative classroom assessments. Take Measured Progress, which partners with states to create state-mandated tests and then turns around to the same districts that will be judged by them and sells them classroom assessments that are conveniently aligned to these tests. It's a brilliant marketing plan. But even when schools don't purchase commercial classroom assessments, teachers often replicate the form and function of the testing industry's tools when they design their own. That's because the testing industry has thoroughly shaped our understanding and uses of assessment tools.

In its current formulation, assessment is forever hostage to its operational imperative: to deny resources and opportunities to most students. I am interested in reimagining classroom assessment outside this rigged system of inequality. I won't pretend that the practical obstacles aren't real. But without a vision of what assessment could look like in a different system, there's no way (and no reason) to find our way around the practical obstacles. It all starts with understanding and rejecting the assessment tool that's perfectly designed for making and maintaining social and economic hierarchies: the scale. Only then can we reimagine assessment for learners in a more inclusive democracy.

2

Our Tools, Ourselves

Hammers, Scales, and Writing Assessment Factories

Feedback. Growth. I was still flabbergasted that these terms could be interpreted so differently by different educators. To Culham (2006), *feedback* meant copying standardized descriptors onto a student's paper. To the principal in the video ("Setting Measures of Academic Progress Goals" 2010), *growth* was the difference between two test scores. To Stiggins (2005), *feedback* was information about how the child had either hit or missed an endless sequence of learning targets.

It wasn't just the standardization embedded in these interpretations that concerned me. I was also beginning to question the assessment tool involved: the scale. After all, Culham's descriptors are aligned to a 5-point scale. The principal's growth scales are determined by the numerical scale of RIT scores. And Stiggins' learning targets are assessed by proficiency scales. I had first encountered scales through grading, and had always intuitively loathed them. But it took me almost a decade of research to understand why.

My first realization was that assessment tools exist within an interlocking system of uses, values, and theoretical foundations. The system that both demands and is demanded by scales is hierarchical in nature, because hierarchies are what scales were designed to create: they rank on a continuum from good to bad or worthy to unworthy. In our hierarchical society, assessment allows us to maintain hierarchy and perpetuate inequality, "scientifically" determining who is worthy of resources and who isn't, who will attend elite institutions and who won't.

Now I understood why the alternative assessment tools I was proposing weren't even recognized as alternatives. I'd say something like, "Conversation is a better 'container' for assessment than a rubric" (Wilson 2006, 2007a, 2007b, 2009), and people would say, "That's nice, but what's the alternative to rubrics?" I'd puzzle earnestly over how to more clearly say, "That *is* the alternative!" But the problem wasn't communication. The problem was that my alternatives didn't include any form of a scale. And if it doesn't include a scale, it can't create and preserve hierarchies.

The tools I was beginning to imagine served the interests of learners who join and form an inclusive democracy, not the interests of students as competitors who race through a sequence of learning targets to vie for access to an increasingly small share of wealth and influence. Silly me. Mine weren't the interests that mattered, and so the existing system spat out my proposed tools.

Are Tools Neutral? How Uses and Values Are Embedded in a Tool's Design Intention

The relationship between assessment tools and their supporting system came into focus as I grappled with why we'd call something like a rubric a "tool" in the first place. I hadn't thought about assessments as tools until some critics responded to my work with variations on this assertion: "Rubrics aren't good or bad. They're *just tools*. It all depends how you use them" (Anson et al. 2012; Spandel 2006; Thompson 2009). The implication was that assessments are neutral. *Don't blame the hammer for smashing your fingernail; blame yourself!* If rubrics are neutral, then responsibility for a bad result is deflected from the rubric to the user. It's a marvelously clever deflection.

However, a deeper range of intentions are designed into a tool from the moment of its conception. For example, a hammer is designed to hit things with more force than my arm and bare hand can muster. This *intent to smash* is embedded in the hammer's shape and materials: a heavy head amplifies the force of the hit and a long wooden handle absorbs the shock of impact and maximizes the speed of the swing. *What* the hammer smashes (a nail, my toe, someone's head) and how effectively it does so are pretty much up to me. But if I intend to use the hammer to do anything other than smash something—to screw a screw, say, or to extract a splinter from under my fingernail—I very quickly learn that my intentions and skill are irrelevant.

A user's skill and intentions matter, but the uses built into a tool's shape and materials—its "design intentions"—matter more. This is why the old National Rifle Association bumper sticker is both true and not true: "Guns don't kill people, people do." The user of the gun certainly pulls the trigger. But the gun embodies its design intention to kill or maim; it was designed to send projectiles hurtling through the air into flesh.

Design intentions, of course, can be political. In an essay titled, "Do Artifacts Have Politics?," Langdon Winner (2000) describes Robert Moses' Long Island parkways. Moses' roads pass beneath beautiful arched stone bridges, some as low as nine feet from the curb. These overpasses appear to be neutral, "just another part of the land-scape" (534). But there is nothing incidental about their height, or lack thereof; as city planner Lee Koppleman put it, "That old son of a gun made sure that buses would *never* be able to use his goddam parkways" (quoted in Winner 2000, 534).

The design of these low overpasses means that members of the public fortunate enough to afford cars or taxis are free to use the Long Island parkways. Those who need public transportation, however (most often the poor and minorities), are denied access. These effects aren't incidental: Moses' well-documented racial and socioeconomic prejudices are embedded in many of his designs (Winner 2000). It doesn't matter whether or not contemporary users of Moses' parkways harbor similar prejudices; they still participate in an infrastructure of inequality. If we pay attention to Winner's insight, we have to rethink our insistence that tools, including scales, are neutral. They have effects that transcend *how* or even *why* we use them.

Gather a bunch of tools together to make a machine, and the effects multiply in the making. In *Understanding Media: The Extensions of Man*, Marshall McLuhan asserts that the technique used to build all machines—the technique of fragmentation—creates its own social effects.

> *In terms of the ways in which the machine altered our relations to one another and to ourselves, it mattered not in the least whether it turned out cornflakes or Cadillacs. The restructuring of human work and association was shaped by the technique of fragmentation that is the essence of machine technology. (1994, 7–8)*

In other words, machines change the way that humans interact, no matter what the machines make. This turns out to be a particularly useful way to understand the effect of rubrics. In fact, rubrics are assessment machines—a collection of tools (scales, traits, performance indicators, and calibrated readers) that have been assembled through the technique of fragmentation. These assessment machines alter all sorts of relationships. To explore McLuhan's point, we'll first examine how the technique of fragmentation increased the production of goods in an industrialized economy. Then, we'll look at the effects of fragmentation on education, and finally, on writing assessment. At that point, the ways in which rubrics alter relationships between readers, writers, and texts should become clear.

Fragmentation in the Factory

The technique of fragmentation involves breaking something into smaller parts. At the beginning of the twentieth century, Frederick Taylor used this technique to standardize factory work and kick off the scientific efficiency movement. Of course, the factory model itself was the product of the fragmentation of work. Taylor's movement just took this a step further.

It worked like this. At Bethlehem Steel, Taylor's assistant documented the individual motions involved in loading each ninety-two-pound slab (or "pig") of iron onto a railroad car, then calculated the time necessary for one man to perform each separate motion. By adding these separate times back together, Taylor's assistant determined that the men *should* be moving the pig-iron four times faster than their current rate of work. This was the infamous time study.

Taylor and his assistant then looked for the fastest, strongest loader, whom Taylor referred to as "Schmidt." Taylor told Schmidt he could earn $.70 a day more by moving four times more iron. But here was the rub: Schmidt would have to follow the steps *exactly* as Taylor and his assistant had worked them out. When Schmidt met this goal, he would train all the other workers just as Taylor had trained him. Workers who refused or were incapable of meeting this goal were "persuaded or intimidated into giving it up" (Taylor 1911, 56). As it turned out, seven of eight men were unable to meet the goal.

Taylor was forced out of Bethlehem Steel soon after, but in 1911, he published the story of Schmidt in *The Principles of Scientific Management*. The book was an instant best seller and Taylor's efficiency techniques became management gospel for decades. Factory workers and teachers alike will recognize Taylor's formula: fragment the work into bits, set standards for increased productivity, train workers to meet the standards, supervise them, measure their performance, reward them if they succeed, and punish them if they fail.

The goal of the factory model and Taylor's further fragmentation and control was to increase profits for owners. As McLuhan (1994) points out, it also changed workers' relationships with home, their work, and each other. Labor in the preindustrial craftsman model had been centered in the home, where family members and apprentices gathered with a sense of ownership over the process and the product. But in the industrial factory model, workers left their homes to stand next to strangers while performing repetitive actions that didn't need to be accompanied by any sense of meaning or purpose. In the film

"Modern Times," Charlie Chaplin's scathing satire, it's no accident that we never learn what is actually being produced at the factory in which Chaplin's character spends his days tightening bolts (and anything resembling a bolt, including the buttons on a woman's skirt). Workers in this model are alienated from their labor, and thus (to borrow Marx's analysis), from their humanity.

Of course, Taylor's ideas on "scientific efficiency" weren't just applied to work in the factory. They were almost immediately applied to education. In 1911, members of the High School Teachers Association (HSTA) of New York City invited an early disciple of Taylor's to speak at their Saturday meeting, and promptly formed a High School Efficiency Committee. Among other efficiency-related tasks, they translated the terms of industrial efficiency (*raw material, product, laborer, executive*) into the terms of the schoolhouse. Pupils were described as raw material on one hand and laborers on another, and teachers were either the workers who turned children into finished products or the executives who oversaw children's labor. Soon, efficiency experts flooded schools around the country to conduct time studies in classrooms, stopwatches and clipboards in hand, while students frantically figured columns of numbers and memorized lists of spelling words like men loading so much pig iron (Callahan 1962).

According to Raymond Callahan (1962), educators adopted Taylor's model so quickly to confer on education the prestige enjoyed by business (vii–viii). The irony? The industrial efficiency movement further undermined the status of teachers by adding several managerial layers to the educational hierarchy, just as it had in the factory. This hierarchy is firmly in place today. Far from where the real work takes place, The National Governors Association and Achieve, Inc. create the standards that define teachers' work. Pearson and Houghton-Mifflin embed these standards into curriculum materials, and Education Testing Service (ETS), Pearson, and Harcourt develop the tests used to enforce them. Closer to the factory floor, curriculum coordinators, principals, and instructional coaches manage teachers, who supervise students in meeting the standards. From the top down, rewards and punishments are doled out according to test results.

Workers (whether we define them as teachers or students) have not benefitted from this reorganization of labor. Their movements have been controlled, and their knowledge, creativity, and experiences have been dismissed. As a result, their relationships to self and work have been undermined. Meanwhile, a growing industry of test makers and scorers, data management companies, textbook publishers, curriculum developers, and instructional coaches have profited, diverting taxpayer money from where it could do the most good.

The Writing Assessment Factory: Calibrated Readers in the Essay Scoring Machine

In a factory model of education, scores are the product of schooling. It follows then, that assessment is the most important step in the educational manufacturing process. Enter the writing assessment factory, powered by the essay scoring machine. We're not yet talking about the digital writing assessment machine. That comes later. Ironically, the technological version of the assessment machine was made in the image of automated humans, which is where our story begins.

Like every machine, the human assessment machine was created by applying the technique of fragmentation. To produce more reliable scores, Diederich and his colleagues (1961) at ETS fragmented quality into factors or traits (ideas, form, flavor, mechanics, and wording), which could be used to narrow readers' focus. Factors or traits, then, are the writing assessment machine's central gear. But a single gear does not a machine make. To manufacture a score, the factor or trait must turn next to its interlocking gear—the scale. Together, the trait and the scale form the mechanical heart of the writing assessment machine.

But to power the trait scale, you still need humans to read the essays. And trait scales by themselves weren't sufficient to standardize readers' readings. So, ETS established the process of reader norming by which they turned human readers into tools. In reader norming sessions, readers are "calibrated" to the rubric and to each other. Readers whose scores don't regularly agree with the others (readers who won't be calibrated) are kicked out. Once you get a calibrated human working in tandem with the trait scale (otherwise known as a rubric or scoring guide), voila! You've got an essay scoring machine.

Corporations such as Pearson, ETS, and Prometric gather these scoring machines together into writing assessment factories, providing the calibration and supervision that churns out scores at a rapid rate. Not surprisingly, these factories tend toward the same abuses as factories in any other profit-driven industry. In 2013, Pearson advertised on Craigslist for scorers to score the Texas Assessment of Knowledge and Skills (TAKS). Teachers were free to apply for the $12 an hour job, but so were applicants with undergraduate degrees in hospitality management (Strauss 2013). It didn't matter if the workers had any experience reading student writing or even working with students. All that mattered was their willingness to be calibrated to a rubric (and each other).

In *Making the Grades: My Misadventures in the Standardized Testing Industry*, Todd Farley (2009) chronicles his fifteen-year career in this largely unregulated industry. In this interview, he explains how the race to create tests for the Common Core State Standards (CCSS) led to even more abuses than normal:

> With the Common Core standards released, all the companies knew all the other companies were racing to finish their tests and products first, so quality became even worse than secondary . . . Subcontractors who had been fired for poor work were rehired; item writers were hired off Craigslist; test developers with neither teaching experience nor test development experience were given full-time jobs . . . companies like Pearson are for-profit enterprises. They want to make money . . . so of course they do a crappy job, because the quality of the work is never anywhere near as important as their desire to make a profit, and there's always too much work and too little time to do it. (Rubenstein 2012)

It is tempting to respond to these abuses with a call for qualified teachers to score high-stakes standardized tests. But when we consider McLuhan's insight, it doesn't matter if writing assessment factories take the shortcuts that Farley documents. It doesn't matter if they hire only teachers. It doesn't matter if the rubrics are created or used outside the factory walls. It doesn't even matter if teachers invite students to create rubrics with them. The rubric and calibration process were developed by the technique of fragmentation to pump out scores, and this purpose is embedded in their design. These machines reorganize relationships between readers, writers, and texts—no matter who uses them, no matter why or how they are used.

Restructured Relationships: Control, Alienation, and the Dismissal of Experience

Control is the factory's major goal—and its central method. The writing assessment factory is no different. It controls readers and writers through separation, alienation, and the dismissal of experience. First, the factory separates readers from writers. Readers are "blind," lest the reader's experience of the writer "contaminate" the scoring process, which is why high-stakes standardized tests aren't scored by students' own teachers. Similarly, students are separated from their readers. Asked to write to an unknown audience, students are given no knowledge of the readers their writing might inspire, inform, persuade, or provoke. Framed as objectivity, this double-blindness is offered as a technical substitute for fairness.

That's not how writing works for me. I never write to a faceless audience; the thought is terrifying. Instead, I write for myself or for people I know. My handpicked imaginary audience usually embodies the concerns of the general audience who might later read my work, but I often include my dad in this group. He isn't a teacher, but he's smart and interested, and if I can write about assessment in ways that keep him engaged, then I'm happy. My knowledge of particular individuals helps me make crucial decisions about what metaphors, examples, arguments, and appeals might resonate.

When I ask others to respond to my writing, I depend on them to have a general sense of my intentions, to know me on some level as a thinker, teacher, writer, and human being. All of this context helps them to help me, especially when my intentions are muddled in the texts I am trying to write. All of this experience and context doesn't contaminate the writing and reading processes; it leads to insight.

It is true that teachers sometimes use grades to punish students *because* they know them. This abuse of power can't be ignored, but banning subjectivity isn't the solution. That would be like saying, "Friends sometimes use what they know about you to hurt you. Therefore, don't ever let your friends know anything about you." That's just getting rid of friendship, not solving a problem that friends sometimes have.

When objectivity is the goal of assessment, writers are alienated from their intentions, from the texts they write, and from their audiences. They cannot establish and carefully consider the relationships (imaginary or real) that propel the act of writing in the first place, that help writers make crucial decisions at every phase of the writing process, and that inform the act of reading. Instead we have to think about how to use our subjectivity and relationships to help students. For example, when I work with resistant writers, it is often my care for them as human beings and my desire to hear what they have to say that convinces them to write at all. Many protest that they don't want to write for the state test—or the more local "common assessment"—because scorers won't care what they have to say. As caring as these scorers might be (and Farley's description of the industry might reveal that their working conditions work against their caring at all), they do not know my students, and so their care is usually too abstract to matter.

As the scoring machine separates readers from writers, it also separates readers from their own experiences. Educational measurement asserts that the great uncertainties of the human sensemaking process—experience, feelings, desires, and ideas—contaminate the reading process for humans. This is balderdash, a lie told to writers by the tools and procedures that students and teachers encounter from the assessment factory. In real life, we can't extricate reading from experience. Without experiences—memories, images, feelings, and ideas—to layer onto words and pull from them, our ability to decode is meaningless.

In truth, there is only one "reader" that doesn't actually make use of subjective human experience in the reading process: the computer. No memories, feelings, ideas, images, or imaginings are involved in the computer's translation from code to action. For human readers, however, these uncertainties are the very stuff and substance of inter-pretation. It's why readers naturally disagree, and why we enjoy shar-ing (and debating) our interpretations of texts with others. When such debate is not a competitive sport or demonstration of superiority, it's another way of sharing experiences.

When we assess writing, we take the use of experience in sense-making several steps further than the average reader. Like any other reader, we comprehend by layering experiences into and from words. We mostly don't even notice this process. The text just makes sense, and we don't stop to wonder why or how. But when we assess, we must become conscious of the experiences we are having of the text. (*Wow, I'm totally not paying attention right now.*) Then, we have to figure out why we're having this experience, a process that is highly speculative. (*I don't think I've zoned out because the text is uninteresting. Maybe I'm trying to figure out where the writer is going, and so I'm distracted from what's actually there. Maybe that's because there's no thesis yet? Or, maybe it's because the text is making me think so much that I can't focus on anything but my own thoughts right now? Or maybe, I'm just tired?*)

All of this happens in real time, buried inside our bodies, as invis-ible as the reading process itself. You might say that we're assessing our experience of the text, not the actual text. The busier we are trying to reconcile this experience with the factors on the rubric, the less we notice the experience at all. And the less we notice our experience, the more likely we are to sacrifice it in the face of other pressures. Instead, we simply look for textual features that tend to produce certain kinds of experiences. (*The thesis is in the wrong place, so the organization is a 3.*)

The pressure in a factory is always to ignore the experiences of workers. It's the owners' profit that matters, after all. That's what leads to exploitation and the dehumanization of workers in a modern economy. This is no less true in a writing assessment factory. Readers who pay attention to their experiences slow down the production of scores. It is faster to scan for a limited set of features and rate them on a scale. Thesis? Score 3. Topic sentences? Score 4.

However, when we ignore our *experience* of those features in favor of rating them, we become inured to surprising uses of language or structure. We might flag the run-on sentence because run-on sentences often confuse readers, but if we paid attention to our experience, we might notice that this particular run-on makes us tense in a way that builds suspense. With experience stripped from the assessment equation, we're stymied in our efforts to make meaning. We're also unable to tell writers the truth about how readers read. And let's be honest: an assessment process that lies about how readers make meaning cannot contribute to the healthy development of a writer. It is, in fact, a de-formative assessment.

Districts, departments, and teachers might not be motivated by profit when they create their own norming sessions for scoring the districtwide common assessment. And classroom teachers who use rubrics can't be calibrated in the same way as a group of scorers at ETS. But they still borrow the techniques and tools of the profit-making machine. Teachers who eschew commercial rubrics in favor of writing their own or even inviting students to make rubrics with them may foster a valuable sense of ownership. But they're still using a tool created for the factory, with vilification of experience as its central design feature. We shouldn't be surprised when a hammer smashes things. And we shouldn't be surprised when scale-based assessments alienate readers and writers from each other and texts, dismissing the experiences of everyone involved.

It's Not You; It's the Tool

The good news? If you feel like you're bashing your head into a brick wall as you try to make assessment work for you, generate data for the common district assessment, prep students for the SAT, and satisfy your institution's accreditation mandates, take heart. It's not you. Mainstream writing assessment tools are incapable of doing what we want them to do. That's because the system that shaped these tools works at cross-purposes with our best intentions as knowledgeable teachers, invested writers, and compassionate human beings who teach for a more inclusive democracy. I desperately wish it were possible to simultaneously honor these intentions and appease the powers that be. The knowledge that you can't serve two feuding masters, however, can be a relief.

The bad news? The alternative assessment tools that I'll introduce—stories and interpretive lenses—can't be substituted for rubrics without causing major resistance or upheaval. That's because they're *not* sponsored by the values or theoretical foundations of our current sociopolitical educational assessment system. We certainly can't change the system overnight. But no system exerts complete control over human thought and activities. Enormous influence, yes. But perfect dominance? There are always gaps and fissures, moments of opportunity in which we can imagine, create, and practice alternatives. Occupying these fissures is important, not just for the work we are able to do within them. As we live and teach out our values within these gaps, our presence creates pressure from within, like melted snow that freezes overnight, quietly opening invisible fault lines in the pavement.

With pressure applied from within, the system is more likely to buckle under its own, top-heavy weight. It's unsustainable. It's inefficient. Most importantly, it was designed to benefit only a few, so it is forever plagued by risk of revolt. The strength of the Opt Out Movement and the recent overhaul of No Child Left Behind point to growing unrest with the system's goals, methods, and effects. The successful efforts of the Seattle teachers to boycott the Measures of Academic Progress test in 2013 testify to the power of thoughtful, organized resistance (Hagopian 2014). If and when the time comes, we'll need more than a different version of the status quo to work toward.

In the meantime, working within these gaps and fissures requires commitment and an understanding of the relationship between tools and the system that sponsors them. Otherwise, it's easy to get sucked into believing, once again, that we can make the existing tools work if we just try hard enough. Once again: we can't. It's like insisting a hammer can be used to screw a screw. Something gets screwed, but it's not the screw.

3

Swapping Scales for Stories

And so, the writing assessment machine grinds away deep within the scoring factory, spewing its toxic cloud of alienation. In the previous chapter, I identified the trait (such as organization or sentence fluency) as the machine's central gear. But the trait must rotate alongside another interlocking gear: the scale. Together with calibrated humans, the trait and the scale power the machine and make the production of scores possible.

Until I looked closely at these enmeshed gears, I hadn't understood that my critique of grades and rubrics had always been a critique of scales and their role in assessment. *What's the student's achievement in this course?* Grades answer this question with two possible scales, laid atop the good–bad binary:

A	B	C	D	F
100%	75%	50%	25%	0%
Good	Pretty Good	OK	Pretty Bad	Bad

Rubrics combine traits with scales and dress them up with descriptors, still laid atop the good–bad binary:

ORGANIZATION

5	4	3	2	I
Well Organized	Organized	Sort of Organized	Not Very Organized	Disorganized
Proficient	Mostly Proficient	Developing	Emerging	Not Proficient
Good	Pretty Good	OK	Pretty Bad	Bad

Scales and their embedded binaries dominate our experience of assessment. They limit our sense of assessment's possibilities, to the point where we struggle to conceive of any assessment tool that doesn't translate to a scale, or any question about a student's performance or growth that can't be answered with a variation on the good–bad binary.

That's a problem for my first alternative assessment tool, the story. Because it's multidimensional, temporal, and contextual, the story doesn't play nice with the scale. To make room for the story, we'll need to question the role played by the scale in enacting educational measurement's historical aims. Then, we'll look to the field of narrative identity, where psychologists have already successfully swapped out the scale for the story as a methodological tool. Their efforts can inform us as we attempt to dislodge the scale from our own theory and practice of assessment.

Why Educational Measurement Loves a Scale, Why Students Don't, and Why Teachers Shouldn't

To ground our discussion in student work, we'll attempt to understand a first grader's visual composition with the scale and then the story. Here's Bob's drawing:

At first glance, Bob's sketch has nothing in common with a researched essay on gun control. It isn't even a text! Teachers of older students, then, might be tempted to dismiss the example as irrelevant. However, this drawing has much to teach teachers of all students. That's because drawings emerge from the same foundational understanding as written compositions. It isn't just that kids who draw practice the skills (such as dexterity and control) that they'll later need to form letters; it's that they're engaged in *representation*, the most basic building block of literacy. You cannot learn to read and write unless you understand that marks on a page can represent experiences, feelings, and ideas. That's why early childhood literacy researchers include *visually viewing and representing* in their definition of literacy, and it's why many teachers encourage children to compose in pictures even as they learn to compose in words (see Ray 2010).

These early drawings turn out to be particularly pertinent when we attempt to put a writer's growth at the center of our thinking about assessment. Later, we'll look at essays composed by older writers. But we need to understand where it all begins if we want to understand and support the growth of the writer through assessment.

First, let's use familiar tools to assess Bob's drawing: traits and a scale. Of course, if we're using a scale, we'll need another drawing by a first grader for comparison. Here's Micah's drawing, alongside Bob's:

Bob   Micah

Three traits occur to me when I see these two drawings side by side: first, neatness of the shading; second, precision of lines and shapes; third, decipherability. Add a scale that aligns to the good–bad binary and we've got three trait scales: messy to neat; imprecise to precise; and decipherable to indecipherable. Now, we simply need to rate each drawing on each trait scale. Here's how the drawings stack up:

Messy   Neat

I	2	3	4	5

Shading Scale

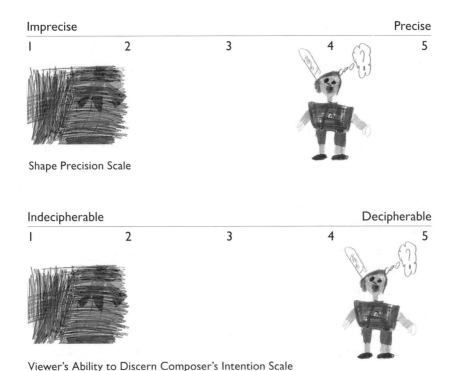

Imprecise   Precise

1	2	3	4	5

Shape Precision Scale

Indecipherable   Decipherable

1	2	3	4	5

Viewer's Ability to Discern Composer's Intention Scale

This exercise feels familiar, even easy. But is it useful? Perhaps, if we wanted to dole out rewards: to give Micah the Art Award for the day, for example or to place Bob in the remedial class and Micah in a class for gifted and talented artists. But what does Bob gain from these assessments, other than the knowledge that Micah is better at shading, drawing shapes, and clearly portraying intentions to a viewer? Nothing.

The scale doesn't help students. But it also doesn't help teachers help students, because the good–bad binary that lies beneath educational measurement's scales limits teachers' understandings. This binary makes quantification possible, because the end of the scale aligned to *bad* is assigned the lowest number and the end aligned to *good* is assigned the highest number. But the binary also takes any description that doesn't align to it off the table.

Take *exuberant*. To put *exuberant* on a scale, we'd have to determine whether it is good or bad, and then find it's opposite—let's say, *restrained*. But is one really good and the other bad? Couldn't both descriptions be either, given the situation? But to conform to the scale, we have to decide; the good–bad binary requires unidimensional judgements. If we can't decide, we simply limit our descriptive possibilities. With words like *exuberant* unavailable, we don't even pause to *think* of Bob's shading in this way. As a result, words that lend themselves to unidimensional judgments (such as *neat* and *messy*) dominate assessment. By flattening our descriptions, scales limit our perceptions.

Scales as Tools: Preserving Social, Economic, and Racial Hierarchies

If assessment is simply a way of asking, "What's going on here?," you would think that assessment tools would enable description, not limit it. And if scales are useless for close, rich, complex description, then you would think that we'd immediately get rid of scales. In fact, you'd think we might consider replacing the field of educational measurement with the field of educational description. But that would be to ignore the most important function of educational measurement and the tools they sponsor.

Scales, of course, make ranking possible. This brings us to the ideological reason that educational measurement loves a scale. Scales were never designed to further the cause of teaching and learning; they were designed to sort citizens into a socially engineered, hierarchical society. Scales join an entire battery of practices (including eugenics) purposely created to enforce racial, ethnic, and economic hierarchies. Educational measurement didn't just incidentally support these efforts: the field emerged to substantiate them. Its tools (scales, rubrics, calibration) are methods of oppression. To be on the losing end of one of these scales is to feel this, and to be a teacher charged with ranking everything your students do is to grapple with the tension between this charge and your desire to engage children in ways that lead to growth.

To understand how something as small and seemingly benign as the scale serves such abominable goals, we have to zoom out to examine the hierarchical vision of societal organization that gives this tool its meaning. This vision has its own history, dating back at least to *The Republic*, in which Plato (2001) describes a society divided into three strata of citizens: bronze, silver, or gold. Gold, of course, represented the ruling class of philosopher kings.

Those privately educated to rule the United States have always studied Plato's *Republic*, and at the turn of the twentieth century, this vision took a decidedly modern turn. With the scientific testing instruments created by educational measurement, psychologists would identify the stuff that schoolchildren were made of and sort them into different classrooms to receive the proper "educational treatments" (Yerkes and Yoakum 1920, 191). The ultimate goal? To preserve and select an elite ruling class on the one hand, and to control, oppress, and even eliminate a class of undesirables on the other. This was particularly urgent at a time when the elite ruling class felt threatened by a wave of immigration from Eastern and Southern Europe.

The overall effort to track citizens into their proper place in the hierarchy was called "mental engineering" (Yerkes and Yoakum 1920, viii). Mental testing was the primary tool used to organize it, and educational measurement was the field created to scientize it. It sounds bizarre, almost like something from a dystopian novel. In fact, *Brave New World* (Huxley 1932) was a direct response to this vision as psychologists rolled it out. But don't take my word for it. Here's the plan in the words of Robert Yerkes, the president of the American Psychological Association, who was responsible for applying psychology to the war effort during World War I and II. You'll notice echoes of Plato's three strata:

> *Before the war mental engineering was a dream; to-day it exists, and its effective development is amply assured. For the present, at least, it is probable that if three grades of Intellect were distinguished in industry, as has been suggested for the school, a very great gain would be made in degree of fitness of the individual for his task, and in his resulting contentment and efficiency. (Yerkes and Yoakum 1920, viii)*

What made this "dream" before the war now "amply assured"? Large-scale standardized testing, which Yerkes and his colleagues (Brigham, Thorndike, and so on) had developed for the war effort to sort recruits into officers and infantrymen.

Although Yerkes claimed that the goal of mental engineering was the "contentment" of all who were tracked, the real goal was to ensure the dominance of the existing elite with the help of their new "science" (see, for example: Yerkes and Yoakum 1920; Wilson 2013). Just as Plato had written himself into the ruling class by establishing gold as the philosopher king, Yerkes and his colleagues (Thorndike, Brigham, Goddard) made sure that their own profession was at the top grade of industry. After all, they had already used their test to grade the intelligence of different kinds of laborers. Only one group of professionals earned an A: engineers (Yerkes and Yoakum 1920, 37). As "human engineers," these psychologists occupied the very top strata of this hierarchy.

The use of mental testing to select an elite ruling class was inextricable from eugenics: an expression of white superiority that sought to cleanse the American breeding stock through immigration quotas and selective breeding techniques, including restrictive marriage laws, institutionalization, segregation, forced sterilization, and restrictive marriage laws (Black 2012). In *Eugenics and Education in America*, Ann Winfield reminds us that eugenics is not an incidental part of our history, nor was it confined to the fringes of twentieth-century society:

> *The efforts to eliminate non-white segments of the population was not the work of some extremist sect in America. Indeed, this war was waged by venerated professors, ivy league universities, wealthy philanthropists and industrialists, educators, armies of social workers and medical professionals, and government officials of all stripes . . . The ultimate eugenic purpose was clear: the prevention of what Franklin Roosevelt called "race suicide" and the creation (within three generations) of a superior Nordic race. It was within this ideological context that our modern form of schooling in the United States was conceived and formed; a fact that historical accountings of education have, for the most part, so far failed to acknowledge. (2007, xviii)*

What is true for education is even more true for educational measurement. After all, educational measurement was an outgrowth of the science of skull measurement. The size of the skull was assumed to correlate to intelligence, and scientists (including Samuel Morton) cultivated skull collections in an attempt to catalog the superiority of the Nordic race (Gould 1981). The field of educational measurement simply moved from measuring the skull to measuring what was assumed to be inside the skull: IQ. Founding members of the field of educational measurement (Robert Yerkes, Carl Brigham, Henry Goddard, Stanley Hall, Charles Davenport) were eugenicists (Zenderland 2001). Their involvement in eugenics wasn't incidental to their work in educational measurement. Instead, educational measurement itself was created as a tool to prove the superiority of the Nordic race and to create gatekeeping tools to select and preserve an elite ruling class. The notion of IQ—a single, stable construct we call "intelligence"—has since been debunked. But the assumption of innate intelligence remains, along with the methods, procedures, and tools designed to measure IQ. Custom-made for confirming and upholding hierarchies, the scale was at the center of these efforts.

Scales also legitimized psychology and education as scientific fields at a time when fields such as astronomy or physiology derived their authority from access to numerous measurement tools. In fact, many of the first educational measurement tools created specifically for schoolchildren used the word *scale*, such as Hillegas' Writing Scales (Lynne 2004). The word *scale* has since fallen out of favor, but its basic design is still firmly embedded in most of our assessment tools today.

Even if we ignore the historical societal context, ranking works against learning. The damage extends beyond the suffering of those crushed at the bottom of the pile. As the most-cited living scholar in the world, Noam Chomsky tops just about any academic scale you'd ever want to devise. But Chomsky himself views all ranking as "very destructive." He explains the lack of ranking at the "Deweyite" school he attended until he was twelve:

> It was an exciting experience, you wanted to be there, you wanted to go. There was no ranking, there were no grades. Things were guided so it wasn't just do anything you feel like. There was a structure but you were basically encouraged to pursue your own interests and concerns and to work together with others. I basically didn't know I was a good student until I got to high school. (Chomsky and Kasenbacher 2012)

Proponents of formative assessment insist that all students need to know exactly where they stand relative to others or to some external standard. That's why Kathy Dyer praises "visually vibrant displays" (2015) of data in her description of feedback as Fitbit. But here's Chomsky's description of the effects of ranking once he got to high school:

> I went to an academic high school in which everybody was ranked and you had to get to college so you had to pass tests . . . High school was totally different—you've gotta be first in the class, not second. And that's a very destructive environment—it drives people into the situation where you really don't know what you want to do. It happened to me in fact—in high school I kinda lost all interest . . . And then I noticed, when my own kids went to school (suburban Boston schools, supposed to be high quality schools), that about the time they were in 3rd grade, they were talking about the smart kids and the dumb kids . . . But the [Deweyite] school I went to just encouraged you to do your best. That's it. No more ranking. (Chomsky and Kasenbacher 2012)

As Chomsky and his teachers at the "Deweyite" primary school knew full well, ranking tools are worse than unnecessary. The comparisons made possible by scales serve the larger goal of a stratified society, not the goal of teaching and learning.

Scales cannot help us describe and support the healthy, sustainable growth of children, but it isn't the scale's fault. It's just doing what we created it to do. If we want to do something different, then we will need to create different tools. We will also need to ask different questions, questions that we've forgotten to ask because they can't be answered with scales.

A Model for New Tools: Narrative Identity Replaces Scales with Stories

Exit the scale; enter the story.

We're English teachers, so this shift should be easy. Stories are our lifeblood. But dragging the story across assessment's well-defended border violates every tenet of educational measurement, so it's a move that may cause anxiety, not to mention outright resistance. Plus, we may have no idea what the story could look like in territory that's been occupied by the scale.

Lucky for us, we're not without a model to learn from. The field of narrative identity has been staging a similar swap since the 1980s. That's when psychological researchers began using the life story as a tool in response to the same dilemma we feel in writing assessment: scales don't help us observe, describe, and communicate complex understandings of identity and growth. We can learn from their story.

Like the field of educational measurement, the study of personality came of age through the use of scales. In the 1930s, personality theorists believed that personality was a stable construct, "reflected in the stable rank-ordering of individuals in their behavior on any given dimension" (Mischel 2004, 1). Traits were the name of the personality game, and they were measured by trait scales: dominant to submissive, emotionally unstable to stable, socially bold to shy, and so on. Personality measurement was much like writing assessment today; your personality might be ranked somewhere on a scale from introverted to extroverted, and your essay might be ranked somewhere on a scale from organized to disorganized (or vice versa).

This shared tool was an historical artifact, as researchers in both fields subscribed to Thorndike's assertion that "everything that exists, exists in some measure" (quoted in Zenderland 2001). In the positivist philosophy of science that dominated the era, a science wasn't really a science unless it could measure what it purported to study. And scales did the trick. Researchers in both fields, then, were actively involved in identifying traits that could easily be scaled, quantified, and tested.

Researchers in personality and educational measurement didn't just share values and tools; in some cases, they were literally the same people. Consider Raymond Cattell, a British psychologist who began his career by studying intelligence, publishing the Cattell Group Intelligence Scale in 1937. In 1938, Cattell was invited to Columbia University by none other than Edward Thorndike, who was already known for his contributions to intelligence testing during World War I. Once at Columbia, Cattell shifted focus from intelligence to personality, creating the sixteen-trait model of personality that helped establish the field of personality studies.

But Cattell never forgot his background in intelligence testing. He embedded intelligence in his model of personality by making reasoning one of his sixteen traits. But more to the point here, he borrowed the methods and tools he'd learned from intelligence testing. Each of Cattell's sixteen traits included a scale ranging from high end to low end. For example, the trait of Warmth included descriptors such as *cool* on the low end and *warm* on the high end. By combining these trait scales with a questionnaire, Cattell created one of the first standardized tests of personality.

Still, Cattell's interest in intelligence testing never waned, nor did the racist assumptions that characterized the establishment of the field of educational measurement. Four years before his death, Cattell publicly defended the patently racist conclusions of *The Bell Curve* (Herrnstein and Murray 1994). When it was published in 1994, *The Bell Curve* was immediately denounced by leading scholars in multiple fields for its shoddy scholarship (it was never peer reviewed) and the way in which its scholarly mistakes always leaned in the direction of prejudice. For example, the authors used their analysis of test data to argue against affirmative action and to call for immigration restrictions and welfare policies that discourage poor women from having babies. In *The New York Times*, Bob Herbert (1994) called the book, "a scabrous piece of racial pornography masquerading as serious scholarship."

Cattell (along with Edward Thorndike's son) signed a letter supporting the book that was published in the *Wall Street Journal* (Gottfredson 1994). The letter asserted that black seventeen-year-olds perform like white thirteen-year-olds on intelligence tests, that the tests themselves are not culturally biased, and these test results shouldn't be seen as a function of socioeconomic status or education. Because genetics is more important in determining intelligence than environment, the letter implied, these results point to racially based genetic deficiencies.

A year before his death, Cattell (1997) tried to set the record straight in an open letter to the American Psychological Association.

He was not racist, he protested, because his interest in eugenics was not in *negative eugenics*, which included practices such as forced sterilization. Instead, his interest was in the practice of *positive eugenics*: encouraging educated people with high IQs of whatever race to have more children. The scientifically supported racism and classism revealed in these letters may have shocked many readers at the end of the twentieth century. But at the beginning of the same century, these views were widespread. More importantly, they actually gave birth to intelligence testing and the scientific field that supported it.

Cattell helped establish the psychology of personality through traits and scales, methods he'd borrowed from his work in intelligence testing. However, the very concept of a personality trait was challenged and almost obliterated in the 1950s. Walter Mischel (2004), the trait's primary challenger, argued that personality is shaped largely by environment, making traits unstable across both time and situation. Personality researcher Theodore Newcomb had noted this as early as 1936. While studying the introversion–extroversion binary at a boys' summer camp, he found that boys who were outgoing in one situation might be quite shy in a different situation. This finding undermined the most basic assumptions of his field and unsettled Newcomb so deeply that he became a social psychologist instead. With Mischel's challenge, the field of personality studies itself experienced a similar identity crisis. Could personality even be studied if traits were neither stable nor meaningful?

When traits reemerged in the 1980s as a legitimate focus of study, psychologist Dan McAdams launched a different challenge from which the field of narrative identity was born. Without denying the existence of traits entirely, McAdams (2006) explained that our identities are not the sum of our personality traits. Traits can only ever constitute what McAdams calls, "*the psychology of the stranger*—a sketch of those broad attributions one might make when first meeting a person" (15). Because traits can never "speak to the problem of meaning in human lives" (17), they cannot answer the most fundamental questions of identity. To speak to the problem of meaning, McAdams argued, psychologists would need to look beyond traits, and they'd need different tools to do the looking.

Introducing the Story as a Tool

McAdams begins *Power, Intimacy, and the Life Story* with a quote from Joan Didion: "We tell ourselves stories in order to live." Then he asserts the central role that stories play in identity development:

> *Like stories in literature, the stories we tell ourselves in order*
> *to live bring together diverse elements into an integrated*
> *whole, organizing the multiple and conflicting facts of*
> *our lives within a narrative framework which connects*
> *past, present, and an anticipated future and confers upon*
> *our lives a sense of sameness and continuity—indeed, an*
> *identity. (1988, ix)*

According to McAdams, we tell ourselves and others stories as we answer the central identity questions identified by Erik Erikson: Who am I? How do I fit into the world? (2006). Constantly under (re)construction, these life stories don't just express our identity. They construct our identity by integrating our experiences, emotions, and personality traits. They also guide our actions by influencing our goals and decisions.

McAdams' description of how we use stories to create our identities deftly avoids determinism. Although we aren't the sum of our personality traits, we also aren't the sum of the things that happen to us. In other words, our circumstances alone don't determine our identity. Instead, we are the sense we make of what happens to us, and this sensemaking happens, in large part, through storytelling.

Of course, we don't just conjure these stories out of thin air. Before we are old enough to form sentences, let alone tell stories, we are gathering the material and tools of our future story making. Our earliest experiences provide the material—key images and characters—that will fill the stories we'll later tell about our lives. These experiences, especially our early attachments, create what McAdams (1988) calls the "narrative tone" of our future stories. In addition, culture provides us story-making tools and materials, including the range of roles available to us, patterns of interaction, prejudices and stereotypes, archetypes and narrative patterns. We don't necessarily import these cultural resources wholesale. But we do interact with them, accepting, rejecting, ignoring, or transforming them.

These stories would be a tool for inquiring into identity. Instead of administering personality trait questionnaires ("Are you more likely to avoid or engage in conversation with strangers at a party?"), psychologists would elicit, listen to, and analyze life stories. These stories were also useful for identify development. According to McAdams (1988), it is through telling and retelling our life story that we forge a coherent sense of self.

Illuminating Complexity: The Story of Bob's Composition

Similarly, the story can become a tool for inquiring into a writer's development, as well as a tool for *creating* a writer's development. In this way, assessment becomes truly formative, *forming* writers even as it helps us understand them and their work. How can we use the story as a tool to understand a writer's development? Let's start with Bob and his drawing.

Using the story as a tool suggests a simple first question: What is the story of Bob's composition? From within this question, the framework of a story—setting, character, and action—gives us multiple avenues for inquiry.

What is the story of Bob's composition?

SETTING:
Where and when does Bob compose? What are the circumstances of his composition: the immediate situation, the rhetorical situation, the cultural backdrop from which he culls materials, purposes, and "forms"?

CHARACTER:
Who is Bob as a composer? What is the story of his development? Why does he compose? What are his intentions? What is he thinking and feeling as he draws? What previous experiences and relationships does he bring to bear on his composing? What relationships does he foster through his composing—and his compositions?

ACTION:
What does Bob do? With what and whom does he interact? What obstacles does he encounter? How does he attempt to overcome these obstacles?

The story of Bob's drawing begins in two separate classrooms: my K–3 Literacy Methods course at the University of Maine at Orono and Megan Dreher's first-grade class in Asa Adams Elementary School. Megan and I were both exploring illustration study with our classes, based on Katie Wood Ray's (2010) *In Pictures and In Words*. We were taken with Ray's insight that writers can learn about their own decision-making process by studying the decisions made by illustrators, and we wanted the college students and first graders to collaborate on a project inspired by this insight.

To understand the many different ways that illustrators depict phenomenon such as perspective and motion, my students and I studied illustrations in children's books. We learned, for example, that some illustrators depict movement by creating multiple versions of the same object in different states of motion. Others create trace lines behind an object. The more we looked, the more techniques we noticed. Then, we studied how authors depict phenomenon like movement through time or multiple perspectives in a single story.

Inspired by some of the choices we noticed in our illustration study, my university students and I composed postcards for Megan's first graders. To practice some of the techniques and to introduce ourselves to our first-grade partners, we depicted something important about our lives on the front of the postcard and wrote about it on the back. For example, Katie drew a large keyhole in the foreground of her postcard with a small, partially obscured figure of a sad-eyed dog looking at the audience through it. On the back, Katie described how her dog, which was very important to her, had gotten locked out of the house the night before.

We sent these postcards to the first graders. They studied our postcards, noticing everything from the techniques in the drawings to the placement of picture, address, message and stamp. When the first graders were ready to compose their own postcards, we visited Megan's class to sit beside our partners while they drew and wrote.

It's the day of our visit, and Megan's classroom is bursting with big people sitting next to little people. Picture Noah, a tall college sophomore, who has just crammed his legs into a teeny chair to sit next to his first-grade partner, Bob. Bob is standing at his desk, a blank 4 × 6 card in front of him, a brown marker in his hand. Bob begins to form the stick figure that you might see hidden behind the scribbles.

As the brown figure takes shape, Bob looks at Noah, grins, and proclaims, "This is you!" He draws a few horizontal lines below the figure of Noah, then picks up an orange marker and moves it enthusiastically up and down over the stick figure. His eyes twinkling with mischief, he giggles and tells Noah, "I just set you on fire!"

Noah reacts with surprise, "Ouch! That hurts!" This reaction seems to increase Bob's glee, until Noah insists, "I don't like being on fire!" Bob pauses, looks at Noah, picks up a blue marker, and scribbles over the entire front of the card. "There!" he announces. "I just dumped a bucket of water on you."

Several understandings emerge from the story of this composition. First, we see that Bob's decision-making process is inextricably tied to his real-time engagement with audience. Within this unique rhetorical context, we can interpret Bob's scribbles as a brilliant decision to convey action through layers that unfold on top of each other: the fire on top of a figure, the water on top of the fire. True, each new layer of action obscures what came before. But that's only a problem if your audience isn't watching you compose, and Noah *is* watching him compose. Similarly, to someone who wasn't there, Bob's lines might be construed as scribbles, showing a lack of control or care. But if we're there, we might see these same lines as evidence of an exuberant hand, mimicking the action he's depicting.

To Bob's intended audience, this exuberance is part of a playful invitation to interact that Noah gladly accepts. ("Ouch! That hurts!" "I don't like being on fire!") Although the content and performance of this invitation is aggressive, Bob eventually responds with empathy to Noah's imaginary pain, indicating a willingness to accommodate even as he provokes. Bob is establishing a complex relationship with his audience: provocative yet responsive. Contrast this with the distant, passive, and obedient relationship with audience promoted by high-stakes standardized testing and its tools. When we consider the development of a writer, which is the more promising relationship?

4

Toward a New Theory of Formative Assessment

Healthy and Sustainable Growth in the Right Direction

Scales are designed to answer two central assessment questions: "How good is this?" and "How does this compare?" These questions turn assessment into a judgmental exercise in ranking. When they dominate our understanding of assessment's aims and methods, they restrict what we look for and therefore what we find. This played out when the scale's allegiance to the good–bad binary forced us to see Bob's drawing as messier than Micah's.

Stories, on the other hand, are designed to answer a radically different question: "What's going on here?" This question opens up assessment's possibilities. Unhinged from the good–bad binary, assessment becomes an inquiry into the aspects of human experience that only stories can illuminate: settings, characters, relationships, actions, reactions, consequences, conflicts, and resolutions. We saw this when the story revealed the exuberance of Bob's engagement with his audience, as well as the logic of his decision to layer the action on top of itself.

The shift from scale to story signifies a corresponding shift in the aims of assessment: from ranking and judgment to understanding and insight. As we learned in Chapter 2, everything has to change around an assessment tool that's truly alternative: aims, uses, values, theoretical foundations, and ultimately, societal organization. Although the scale maintains a hierarchical society by selecting a ruling elite, the story serves the interests of an inclusive democracy by illuminating experience. As John Dewey pointed out, the only reason to prefer democracy is its potential for improving the experience of the greatest number of people (1938). An assessment tool that illuminates experience doesn't *ensure* that we'll create a more inclusive democracy. But it becomes more difficult to impose suffering and oppression when we're paying attention to the experiences of others.

With a new aim that serves a different vision of society, our new assessment tool needs a new theoretical foundation. Educational measurement theory won't do. Any tool designed to further the cause of democracy cannot be supported by a theory that vilifies experience in the name of objectivity for the ultimate purpose of maintaining hierarchies. And so, concern for experience must be the foundation of a new assessment theory and practice. I don't just mean an *attitude* of concern on the part of individual teachers who assess students' writing. Concern for experience needs to be writing assessment's guiding principle and the central design intention of its tools.

We don't have to construct such a theory from scratch. John Dewey's philosophy of experience in education is the foundation for this book's central idea: The most important consideration is not whether an assessment is valid or reliable. Instead, what matters most are the consequences the assessment has in the child's experience of writing. As we shift our attention from objectivity to experience, our understanding of growth will shift, too. To find the grounds for growth, we'll examine one more drawing, composed by four-year-old Jonah. What we learn from Jonah about growth will become a new interpretive lens to apply to the stories uncovered by our new assessment tool. Only then will *form*ative assessment for teaching and learning become a real possibility. After rejecting the use of scales, which con*form* students to their place in a stratified society, we'll finally discover how the story can *form* writers in healthy ways.

Dewey's Philosophy of Experience

For Dewey, concern for experience wasn't just about kindness or a moral imperative, although these are certainly enough to recommend it. Concern for experience was also the theoretical basis for teaching. Dewey believed that to make decisions about materials and activities, teachers must understand students' experiences and carefully structure them toward growth. To do so, he insisted, we need a better understanding of what experience is and how it works—a philosophy of experience.

In *Experience and Education*, Dewey (1938) asserted that we are always experiencing the world, making sense of the environment through our physical senses, previous experiences, emotions, thoughts, values, and reflection. This was a gentle reprimand to those of Dewey's followers who had substituted exciting experiences for boring lectures without bothering to ask, "Exciting to what end?" The problem, Dewey explained, isn't that students who sit passively during a boring lecture don't have experiences while students involved in a "lively" hands-on activity do. Rather than asking, "*Is* the student having an experience?," Dewey wanted teachers to ask, "What *kind* of experience is the student having?"

Dewey identified two broad categories of experience that should matter to educators: "educative" and "miseducative." To distinguish between them, he introduced two criteria. The first involves agreeableness. An agreeable experience is educative when it leaves the student receptive to future learning experiences, and a disagreeable experience runs the risk of bing miseducative if it makes a child "callous" (13) to future learning. Contemporary literacy educators such as Nancie Atwell (2007), Penny Kittle (2013), and Kelly Gallagher (2009) take Dewey's warning about callousness to heart when they argue for choice in reading. There's been no gain, they insist, if students forced to read *The Scarlet Letter* resort to SparkNotes and learn to hate reading.

Better to guide choice and introduce various classics as students are interested and ready for them.

Although an agreeable experience is more likely than a disagreeable one to leave a student receptive to future learning experiences, the solution isn't simply to make everything fun. According to Dewey, a "vivid, lively, and 'interesting'" activity might still lead to growth in the wrong direction (1938, 14). His second criterion is where things get really interesting—the *direction* of a student's growth. To be truly educative, Dewey insisted, an experience must lead to growth in the right direction.

Applying Dewey's Criteria to Assessment: Educative or Miseducative?

Dewey's criteria for educative experiences are typically applied to pedagogy (assignments, activities, materials). But there's no reason we shouldn't apply them to assessment. After all, a child's experience in school is increasingly shaped by high-stakes standardized tests, districtwide benchmark tests, common assessments, diagnostic tests, and classroom-based assessments. In 2015, the Council of Great City Schools surveyed the 66 largest urban districts in the United States and estimated that eighth graders in participating schools spent an average of 25.3 hours during the 2014–2015 school year taking mandated assessments (9).

Although drastic enough to cite in the Obama administration's proposal to cap standardized testing at 2% of classroom time, this estimate is probably quite low (Serrano 2015). It doesn't include standardized assessments mandated by individual schools, or quizzes and tests chosen or created by individual teachers. And it doesn't count time spent preparing for or administering them. This last omission is particularly relevant for elementary teachers, who regularly give an array of individually administered standardized literacy assessments. For example, a single first-grade student might spend only ten minutes taking a running record, but her teacher will spend hours administering them to each of the twenty first graders in her class. Of course, a running record is just one of many assessments an elementary teacher might give on a monthly or even weekly basis. One third-grade teacher in my district told me that she had recorded the mandated assessments she had given in her classroom in 2006–2007: they took a quarter of the school year. Assessment constitutes such a major portion of students' experience in school that it's fair we apply a Dewey—an analysis.

Let's return to the second-grade classroom we visited in Chapter 1 to determine whether their celebration of assessment data is educative or miseducative. After joining the principal in an enthusiastic chorus of "Data is *fabulous*!," students cheer wildly at the news that they've grown 10 points. It's a scene that perfectly embodies Rick Stiggins' vision for formative assessment: "the entire emotional environment surrounding the prospect of being evaluated must change . . ." and assessment procedures must "promote hope." The mood in the classroom is happy, confident, *agreeable*. The students are primed—for their next discussion of test data. In this sense, the experience may be agreeable enough to leave the students open to future experiences, meeting Dewey's first test. Of course, things get more complicated when we consider which experiences the celebration of data leaves students open to—math and reading or discussion of test data—but we'll take it on face value for now.

Growth in the Right Direction: The Lesson of Foie Gras and *The Biggest Loser*

But what about Dewey's second test? Does this celebration of scores lead to growth in the right direction? The entire experience is framed as *growth*: the chart at the front of the room proclaims, "It's About Growth!" and the principal asserts, "We're going to talk about your growth." The revelation that students have met their growth targets would seem to confirm *growth in the right direction*. If we define growth as *an increase in the amount of something*, then technically speaking, this experience has met Dewey's second test.

However, technical definitions of *growth* don't cut it when we're talking about the learning and development of a human child. A claim that *scores* have grown is different than a claim that the *writing* has grown, much less a claim that the *writer* has grown. Mina Shaughnessy's research demonstrates how conventions previously mastered tend to fall apart when students attempt more complicated grammatical structures, rhetorical situations, or genres (1977). This means that risk-taking (one indication of growth) may result in scores that fail to identify actual growth. Likewise, the essay might grow (technically speaking) even when the *writer* doesn't. Consider the student who dutifully corrects all the issues pointed out on the first draft of the first essay of the year, leading to a perfect second draft. Then she makes all those same mistakes in a subsequent essay. The scores from draft to revision of the first essay have grown. Did the writer grow? Maybe not so much.

To imagine what Dewey means by growth in the right direction, we'll first need to conceptualize growth differently. Etymology points the way. After all, the word *growth* doesn't come from the world of numbers. Its Old Norse, High German, and Middle English roots are planted firmly in the world of living organisms. In this world, the word *growth* conjures up unfurling green seedlings and toddlers whose feet have outgrown their winter boots, and, in a more modern psychological context, the child who has finally mastered her fear of the dark. These images of growth underscore Dewey's insistence on *experience*, which shifts our attention from the world of data charts to the world of living beings. *It is the person who grows, after all.*

The natural world supports Dewey's reminder that not all growth is cause for celebration. In medical terminology, a *growth* refers to a tumor. And let's not forget gavage, the practice of force-feeding a duck, causing rapid growth that is good for foie gras but very, very bad for the duck. This emphasizes Dewey's insistence that the important question isn't simply "Has there been growth?" but also "Has there been growth in the right direction?"

Our attempts to determine educational growth that's healthy is complicated by a societal obsession with superficial markers of growth. Perhaps nowhere are the resulting ironies more absurd or tragic than in *The Biggest Loser*. For over a decade, morbidly obese contestants have competed to lose as much as thirty pounds a week. Each episode is driven by the show's culminating act of numerical assessment, the weigh-in. Our technical definition of growth is the name of the game, with a clever twist: gain as loss. Contestants step onto the scale in front of a live studio audience while the totals are tracked from week to week. The contestant who loses the most wins the season and is dubbed "The Biggest Loser."

If we're just looking at the numbers, the results are truly impressive. In 2009, Danny Cahill won season 8 by losing 239 pounds. But, according to former contestants (and even some trainers), these feats of loss are achieved through methods that cause physical and psychological harm: severe diet restriction, extreme exercise, and constant shaming. During the show, contestants lose hair, pass out, break down emotionally, and experience memory loss. Back at home after the final weigh-in, most contestants gain weight back (sometimes more than they lost), suffer permanent declines in their metabolisms, confront liver problems, and deal with joints ruined from hours of exercise a day (Kolata 2016). The biggest winner? The network. Contestants *are* the biggest losers, as statistically extrapolated growth does not always indicate healthy and sustainable growth.

I need to pause and briefly explore a concern I have with relying so much on Dewey's phrase "growth in the right direction." The word *right* rubs me the wrong way. It fits too neatly into the discourse of educational reform, which is dominated by the search for "best practices" that will "scale up" and guarantee success wherever they're implemented. It's a tiny leap from *best practices* to *right practices*, and both phrases top a slippery slope that plummets to a mandate. No matter how brilliant I think any practice might be, the practice of mandating practices doesn't work (Wilson 2006, 2010). So, I don't want readers to think that *growth in the right direction* means that I'm proposing One Right Assessment Tool, or implying that my proposal will work for everyone.

With such major reservations, why use the phrase in the first place? First, we can't use the phrase without a discussion of aims. Remember our poor duck, pumped full of food until its liver is ten times its normal size? If our aim is to sell or eat foie gras, perhaps that's growth in the right direction. If our aim is for the duck to thrive, that's definitely not growth in the right direction. So, if I use the phrase *growth in the right direction*, I have to be transparent about my primary aim: the healthy and sustainable growth of young writers within an inclusive and equal democracy.

That last part of that phrase, *within an inclusive and equal democracy*, matters to me. Democracy is foundational to Dewey's philosophy of education, and it's foundational to my philosophy of writing assessment. That means that I *do* privilege some kinds of growth over others, and my assessment tools embody these values. For instance, some teachers value compliance, and their writing assessments focus on how well writers follow directions. I value democracy and equality, which requires citizens who are active and informed decision makers who aren't constantly ranking and being ranked. For me, this is the right direction. When it comes to enacting this direction, there's no One Best Way. But there certainly are tools that lead us in the wrong direction, such as the scale, which moves us toward hierarchy and away from an inclusive and equal democracy.

Still, the fact that I unabashedly privilege growth that supports democracy doesn't mean that there's one way to think about or nurture this kind of growth. My assessment tools will focus on the growth of a writer's decision-making capabilities. Just as there might be several dozen different diets suitable for a child's healthy and sustainable growth, there might also be several dozen different assessment tools that observe and support decision making.

A Writer's DNA

What Jonah Can Teach Us About Growth in the Right Direction

If growth can't be extrapolated from the scores, where should we look for it? Given Dewey's focus on the person, a biologically inspired metaphor is in order. My understanding of DNA peaked in tenth grade, but I still find the concept of an inheritable blueprint that interacts with environment helpful when considering how a writer's growth unfolds over the course of a lifetime.

Of course, there are significant limits to the DNA analogy, and we'll get at least some of those out of the way right away. Writing isn't genetic in the sense of green eyes or male pattern baldness, emerging without effort or instruction. Writing requires some of both. And writing isn't heritable in the sense of unattached lobes, present in some people's genes but not others. It's more in line with Chomsky's notion of a language organ (2000)—part of our human "biological endowment" (4) that expresses itself in a multitude of ways within different linguistic and cultural environments. Every child inherits the same principles of language: plunk the child within a Swahili-speaking family, and he'll learn Swahili. Plunk him in a Japanese-speaking family, and he'll learn Japanese (8).

The DNA analogy affirms that we all have what it takes to compose even before we learn to write; we just need a suitable environment in which writing will develop and express itself. Without suitable environmental stimulation, ability can atrophy. And with too many of the wrong environmental factors, it can be damaged. But what it takes to write is not, to borrow Stephen King's phrase, "unusual equipment" (2000, 18). That's the good news. The bad news is that what it takes to write is so basic that it's difficult to see. In fact, it doesn't involve language at all, or, at least not in the way we might think. That's why we get into trouble when we try to measure a writer's growth. We're looking in the wrong place.

A writer's DNA involves our expressive, curious, creative, and social nature. It allows us to make decisions based on a particular set of relationships as we work with a medium. The medium can vary: words, paint, movement, sound, landscapes, numbers, the structure of buildings or bridges. But that decision-making core—and all the relationships that constitute it—has to grow for the writer, artist, dancer, musician, gardener, architect, or engineer to develop. Unfortunately, this decision-making core gets lost when we're so busy looking at the text.

DNA: A Metaphor for Growth

- The ends are in the beginnings; we all have what it takes to write even before we learn to write.
- Our decision-making core is guided by relationships between intention, audience of self and others, and the exploration and transformation of a medium.
- Growth expresses itself through and in supportive environments.
- A lack of environmental stimulation can cause atrophy.

It isn't that language isn't important to writing, or that we shouldn't think carefully about the text itself. But we have to think about the text in relationship to the writer and all the decision-making relationships that govern the act of writing. Surely, it's important for the writer to grow in her understanding and ability to use language. But when we're assessing for growth, we need to see the text as a window into the functioning of a writer's decision-making core. Otherwise we're just ranking or pronouncing the text good or bad, not using assessment to understand or support a writer's growth.

Let's look for that expressive, curious, creative, and social decision-making core in Jonah, who is four years old. He was born prematurely, so he's small for his age, and he can't yet write his name. But when I consider the writers of all ages I've worked with (my own children from birth to adolescence, my students from junior high to graduate school to seventy-two-year-old "Grandma" in adult education), I realize that I've been trying to nurture the same relationships that are alive and healthy in Jonah. We'll get to the language part later. Like I said, it's important. But the language part can't develop as it needs to unless the decision-making core grows alongside it.

Here's Jonah's drawing:

There's not much we can learn about growth from just looking at this drawing. To use it as a window into Jonah's decision-making core, we'll need our new assessment tool, the story. Just as Noah sat beside Bob while he drew, I sat beside Jonah and talked with him as his drawing took shape. (It's worth noting here that the Latin root of *assessment* is *assidere*, "to sit beside.") As with many stories, there's a backstory. Two minutes before Jonah began working on the drawing I've shared here, he drew a simple closed shape on a small pad of paper. When I asked him to tell me about it, he explained that it was a horse leg, and told me that he was a cowboy. Then, as he drew a cowboy hat next to the horse leg, he described the horses that he and his siblings owned. His brother's horse, he reported, had died while walking in a field. At this revelation, Jonah ripped off the sheet with the horse leg, crumpled it up, threw it away, and started the drawing you see. I've represented it in stages below to mirror how it took shape alongside our conversation.

Maja: Can you tell me about this?

Jonah: I forgot what it is called. It looks like . . . a flashlight!

Maja: It does look like a flashlight! There's that white part, that looks like the light coming out of the flashlight!

Jonah: But it's not a flashlight. It's the kind of thing that pokes. If you touch this side, it pokes. (Jonah points to the spiky shape in the upper right hand corner of the drawing.) It pokes you. Ouch! It pokes, see? (Pause, as Jonah continues to point.) It's a porcupine! (Pause.) Have you seen the movie, *Shadow*?

Maja: No, can you tell me about it?

Jonah: (Speaks too softly to be heard.)

Maja: Does the movie mean a shadow like the shadow on this table of your cup?

Jonah: No, no! Shadow is, a, like, no, Shadow is a dog! There's a porcupine in it! But Shadow doesn't get porced by the porcupine. (Jonah's finger repeatedly taps around the outside edge of the shape he has drawn.) This is a porc, porc, porc! (Pause.) This doesn't look like a porcupine. It looks like a flashlight. (Jonah picks up his pencil and draws lines that mimic the tapping of his finger moments ago.)

Jonah: *Now* it looks like a porcupine. What does it look like to you?

Maja: It looks like a flashlight-porcupine!

Jonah: It is!

Jonah: This is a bridge. Something is falling on it. On its head. It's a horse! The horse is falling on its head!

Maja: Ouch! Where's the horse?

Jonah: This is the horse. The horse is on the bridge. But the bridge doesn't . . . Actually, this isn't a bridge. It's an elevator. The horse was in an elevator. The horse lived in the elevator. The horse lived in *this* elevator. See, the horse is behind here.

Jonah: It's raining. Doesn't it look like it's raining?

Maja: Yes, I can see the raindrops right there!

Jonah: Now the porcupine is getting all wet. The porcupine lives on the snow. That's a hatchet in the snow. (Points to the *V* shape at the bottom of the picture.) And the porcupine fell on the hatchet. This is the part where the porcupine fell on the hatchet. He was dead. But not the horse.

The relationship between Jonah, his intentions, his audience, and the medium drive his decisions and revisions. When we try to determine Dewey's notion of growth in the right direction, these are the relationships we need to look at.

Decision-Making Relationships Between Jonah, His Intention, His Audience, and His Medium

Intentions

Shaped by his experiences and his wishes, Jonah's intentions are the starting point for his drawing. To begin, Jonah draws on a movie he loves: *Homeward Bound*. He originally calls the movie *Shadow*, but Shadow is actually the name of one of the dogs in *Homeward Bound*. Shadow's friend Chance gets "porced" by a porcupine in the movie, thus giving Jonah the subject of his drawing.

In the second half of the drawing, Jonah brings in another subject from his experience, a horse. (Remember the death of his brother's horse, which he told me about as he drew a horse leg?) As two different parts of his experience interact in his drawing, Jonah sets up a choice: killing off the porcupine or the horse. ("This is the part where the porcupine fell on the hatchet. He was dead. But not the horse.") Jonah could not control the death of his brother's horse in reality. But he can control the medium. Mixing up his experience with his wishes through the medium allows him to fictionalize and rewrite his first experience with death. He uses the medium, then, to express and transform experience.

Audience of Self and Others, Real and Imagined

Throughout the drawing, Jonah's relationship with his audience is very much alive and helps him make decisions. He is his own first audience, and as he tries to tell me that he is drawing a porcupine, he realizes that what he has made looks, to him, like a flashlight. ("It looks like a flashlight. But it's not a flashlight." And later, "This doesn't look like a porcupine, it looks like a flashlight!") Throughout, he wants to know what I see in his drawings. ("What does it look like to you?" and "Doesn't it look like it's raining?") When we both confirm that what's on the page doesn't match his intention, he doesn't seem frustrated or disappointed. He simply notes the mismatch. ("But it's not a flash-light. It's the kind of thing that pokes.") In fact, he expresses a sense of delight when I proclaim that it looks like a mix of his intention and his perception. ("It looks like a porcupine-flashlight!" "It is!"). He calmly keeps working to bring the drawing in line with his intention. ("*Now* it looks like a porcupine.")

Medium

If you work with any medium, you quickly learn that the medium has a mind of its own. The Dutchman's Pipe you planted to create a living wall literally takes over the entire garden. The watercolors bleed into the grain of the paper. You can spend a lot of energy trying to impose your mind on the medium. Something interesting can result from this tension. But sometimes, mastering the medium means bending your mind to it, not the other way around. Struggle and acquiescence are both key.

Jonah spends much of his time trying to get the shape he has drawn to look more like a porcupine. At first, he doesn't know how to do it. Ultimately, he has to put down his pen and repeatedly poke the side of the flashlight to show me how the porcupine "porcs"; it is only without the pen that he finds the movement necessary to draw the quills. When one medium fails, motion and talk fill the gap and help him bring something new to his manipulation of the pen. When Jonah realizes that the bridge he's drawn looks more like an elevator, however, he lets the medium master him. ("Actually, this isn't a bridge. It's an elevator.") In this case, the medium shapes as much as expresses Jonah's intention.

Assessing Growth in the Right Direction

HOW ARE THE WRITER'S *INTENTIONS* ENGAGED THROUGHOUT THE WRITING PROCESS?

- What motivated the act of writing?
- What was the interplay between internal and external (and intrinsic and extrinsic) motivations?
- What influenced the writer's intentions as she wrote?
- How were big and small decisions influenced by the writer's intentions?

HOW DOES THE WRITER USE HER SENSE OF AUDIENCE (SELF AND OTHERS, REAL AND IMAGINED) TO MAKE DECISIONS THROUGHOUT THE WRITING PROCESS?

- What is the author's relationship with readers—and her understanding of them?
- How does the writer's relationship with her audience (self and others, real and imagined) affect her writing process, in positive and negative ways?
- How does the writer negotiate her relationship with audience (self and others, real and imagined) to solve problems, push forward, or revise?

continues

Stories Need Interpretive Lenses

In Chapter 3 we used the story as a tool to assess Bob's drawing, which illuminated the layers of action (water dousing the fire consuming the figure of Noah) as a clever decision given his audience's presence and participation. Similarly, using the story as a tool to assess Jonah's drawing revealed the active relationships between intentions, audience, and medium that constitute a writer's decision-making core. When we used the trait scale as a tool to assess Bob's drawing, however, we were forced to judge it as "messy" and "indecipherable." If we had used the trait scale to assess Jonah's drawings, we would likely have come to similar judgments.

On its own, the story can't generate insight. Although it made the setting, motivations, and action of Bob and Jonah's compositions available to us to us, interpretation was still required. Just as the trait and the scale are twin gears in the assessment factory's scoring machine, the stories and the interpretive lenses work together to create understanding and insight.

Stories support and inspire a multitude of interpretations. For example, the interpretive lens I used in analyzing Jonah and Bob's drawings involved the concept of a writer's DNA: the relationships between writer, intention, audience, and medium that make up a writer's decision-making core.

The lens I've proposed for looking at the growth of a writer's decision-making relationships has potential as a kind of primary lens for teachers who work with writers. But it is one of dozens of possible interpretive lenses that would yield useful insights. For example, we might interpret the violence and humor in Bob's depiction of Noah through a gendered lens. Tom Newkirk (2000) has written about the performance of masculinity in the writing of young boys, arguing that these gendered performances are often penalized and viewed as deficits, when they could be used as resources for the development of literacy. It is impossible not to think of Bob's relationship with Noah when Newkirk asserts,

> It is a mistake, I feel, to automatically equate boys' use of violence in writing with any desire to be vicious or sadistic. To do so ignores the possibility that "violence" can be mediated, viewed with humorous detachment, and appropriated for a variety of non-violent ends, including the maintenance of friendship. (2000, 295)

As a woman who has both experienced and studied men's violence against women, I am aware of my own tendency to react negatively to the presence of violence in the fantasy life of boys. I maintain that it is important to confront and question violence, but I also believe that it is important not to read my own fears into a child's exploratory play in ways that demonize the child. I purposely brought Newkirk's insights into my interpretive lens when I described Bob's interaction with Noah, highlighting the ways in which Bob honored Noah's protest even after he inflicted imaginary pain.

Such interpretive diversity, which depends on the experiences, background, and preferences of the assessor, is unfair if we want to use assessment to award or withhold resources for the purpose of separating students into different strata in a hierarchical society. We can't have one assessor who would award a scholarship to a student while another assessor would bar that student from going to college in the first place, lest the stability of the hierarchy be undermined.

However, I'm not just arguing that we need an alternative assessment tool. I'm arguing that we need to change assessment's aims, uses, and theoretical foundations as well as the interests it serves.

	Scale-Based Assessment for a Stratified Society	Story and Growth-Based Assessment for an Inclusive Democracy
Aims	• Judgment • Ranking	• Understanding • Insight
Uses	• Rewarding or punishing students, teachers, school districts • Awarding or withholding society's resources • Maintaining hierarchies	• Forming writers in healthy ways • Informing teachers to help them design educative writing experiences
Theoretical Foundations and Values	• Educational measurement theory • Positivism • Objectivity • Behaviorism	• Dewey's philosophy of experience: growth in the right direction • Rosenblatt's transactional theory • Constructivism

Tools and Techniques	• Scales (embedded in rubrics and scoring guides)
	• Traits (embedded in rubrics and scoring guides)
	• Descriptors
	• Fragmentation
	• Reader calibration
	• Controlled writing conditions (timed, standardized prompt, restricted access to resources including conversation)
	• Blind rating
		• Story of the writer and the writing: gathered through conversation, observation
		• Interpretive lenses
		  o A writer's DNA (growth)
		  o Gender
		  o Cultural
		  o Psychological
		  o All the interpretive lenses we might use to understand literature and/or human beings

continues

	Scale-Based Assessment for a Stratified Society	Story and Growth-Based Assessment for an Inclusive Democracy
Central Assessment Question(s)	• How good is this (or a part of this)? • How does this compare to others?	• "What's going on here?"
Understanding of Growth	• An increase in scores	• Healthy expression and development of a writer's DNA: interaction between a writer, her intentions, her relationship with her audience (self and others)

Response to Writers	• Feedback
	  ○ Praise for meeting standard
	  ○ Criticism for not meeting the standard
	  ○ Suggestions for how to meet the standard
		• Interaction
		  ○ To support and develop the writer's intentions
		  ○ To support and develop the writer's relationship with audience (self and others)
		  ○ To support and develop the writer's relationship with language in light of her relationships with intention and audience (self and others)
		  ○ Description of reader experience—but only when it supports previous considerations

In scale-based assessment for a stratified society, my conversation with Jonah doesn't look like assessment. I didn't set a prompt for Jonah or otherwise control the conditions of his composition. I didn't explain the target he should aim for and show him the tool I'd use to determine whether he'd hit or missed that target. I didn't compare his work to anyone else's. I didn't judge any aspect of his drawing. I didn't praise Jonah's work for hitting a learning target, nor did I criticize him for missing it. I didn't give him suggestions for better meeting the standard next time.

Jonah and I simply interacted as he drew. I watched him, we talked, I asked him a few questions, he asked me a few questions. There was little "feedback" involved, which I only offered when he specifically asked for it. I told the story of how Jonah relied on his intentions, his sense of audience, and his interaction with the medium to make decisions. But that story remained thoughts and impression at the time; I only told the story later as I wrote about it.

This may not look like assessment, but it is. Our assessment tool, the story, can't be displayed in a chart or something like a trait scale. But the story requires access to a range of considerations: backstory, character, motivations, interactions, conflicts, resolutions. Sitting beside and talking to Jonah gave me this access. What I looked for (and what I saw) was a function of the interpretive lenses I used, the growth lens in particular.

Our focus on growth requires us to see our students as all ages wrapped into one. In Dewey's philosophy of experience, this is the principle of *continuity*, in which every experience lives on in future experiences. The writer's decision-making core, then, is a veritable cauldron of experiences: the sense the student has made of hundreds of previous experiences with his intentions, audiences, and the medium of language itself, all of them reacting to each other and blending together.

Assessment helps me to understand this bubbling mix. That's important because everything we do together in a semester—every assignment, conversation, activity, and assessment—gets thrown into the pot and must interact with what came before. Time plays a curious role in our central assessment question, then: "What's going on here?" The word *here* normally points to the here and now, to this particular moment. However, the older a writer is, the more experiences have contributed to the here and now. That's a curiosity that our assessment tool, the story, is well suited to accommodate. In narration, the front story often makes no sense without the backstory. Story-based assessment, then, can handle temporal fluidity in a way that scale-based assessment cannot.

To make Dewey's principle of the continuity of experience more concrete, I remind myself that each eighteen-year-old who enters my class was once a four-year-old like Jonah and may someday live to be seventy-two like Lucille, aka Grandma, a student at the adult education program where I started my career. And I think of my two children and the particular perspective I have gained from interacting with their decision-making cores from the beginning. To honor the range of ages needed for a growth perspective, I'll share stories about the conversations and interactions I've had with my students and with my own children in the next few chapters.

I'm not claiming that these kinds of conversations, observations, storytelling, and interpretations are new or somehow unique. I believe they happen in classrooms every day. I am claiming that *these conversations, observations, storytelling, and interpretations are assessment*. They can help us figure out growth in the right direction, form writers in healthy ways, inform our instruction, and further the cause of a more equal and inclusive society.

5

Assessment Phoropters

Interpretive Lenses
That Illuminate Growth

The first time we used the story as an assessment tool, it illuminated Bob as he set a stick-figure Noah on fire. When the actual flesh-and-blood Noah protested, Bob doused him with blue-marker water. Next, our story tool showed Jonah as he struggled to make his flashlight-porcupine more like a porcupine than a flashlight. Examining these stories with our growth lens revealed a healthy decision-making core at work in both children, with decisions shaped by their relationships with their intentions, their audience, and the medium.

It's time to move from Bob and Jonah's drawings to the texts composed by older writers, but we'll take our story tool and growth lenses with us. Because these tools are essentially invisible, it can be helpful to visualize the role that interpretive lenses play in assessment. Toward that end, picture an antique Phoropter.

It sounds like some kind of vicious winged dinosaur, but it's actually a very steam-punkish-looking (but frequently used) ophthalmologist's device. Modern Phoropters often have casings that hide the swiveling mechanism, so that's why we're looking at an antique. At the top and center is a primary lens pair, with a series of secondary lenses swiveling behind. By rotating the secondary lenses past the primary lens pair, the ophthalmologist can determine a patient's prescription. For our metaphoric purposes, however, the lenses in our Phoropter aren't about prescription; they're about interpretation. Each lens brings some objects and phenomenon into view while obscuring others.

These rotating lenses are helpful for sensemaking (which is what interpretation is all about) because reality is a tangle of details that are impossible to perceive all at once, at least consciously. This is as true for the details in a story as it is for the details on a visual plane. For example, here are two details I omitted from the story of Jonah's composition: sunlight illuminated the table while he worked, and Jonah's voice got raspy at one point in our conversation until he coughed. Although true, these details didn't make the cut because they didn't make sense within the growth lens that I was using to tell the story. In other words, an interpretive lens focuses our attention on details that fit together in some systematic way, helping us make meaning from a mess of truths. This is why we often revisit old stories as we learn a new interpretive frame; details that had receded as insignificant at the time now come back into view as part of a significant fact pattern.

Like any metaphor, the Phoropter metaphor has its limits. The useful part of the analogy is the Phoropter's interpretive dexterity. It emphasizes the assessor's active role in making meaning, making assessment unsuitable for the unskilled labor and profit pyramid allowed by the factory. And it underscores the possibility of multiple perspectives. By privileging sight, however, the Phoropter metaphor obscures other forms of perception that help us interpret students' growth, such as embodied knowledge and emotional and social intelligence. We'd be wise to remember that interpretation doesn't just allow us to *see;* it allows us to hear and feel and think and know and relate in all the ways that human beings make sense of their experiences.

Of course, we don't just use lenses for interpretation after a story has been told; these lenses actually influence the way we tell stories in the first place. We each build and internalize certain lenses based on our experiences, ideas, and values, which means that we pay attention to certain details without being aware that we're interpreting at all. For example, the growth lenses are integral to my vision. They feel part of my eyeballs, not some set of lens that I put on and take off again. Until I observed Jonah and Bob's drawings five years ago, I hadn't articulated or even been able to see how these lenses affected my own vision. Still, they're lenses I've been developing for most of my teaching career.

As I write this chapter, I'm sitting in front of a stack of examples pulled from twenty-one years' worth of reading and responding to student writing, including student-teaching. As I look through them, I can see that even in those early years, I was concerned with my students' relationships with their intentions, their audiences, and the medium of language. Without mandated rubrics, I may not have had cause to articulate the beliefs and ideas behind my practice. But, here we are.

The Trait Scale and Growth Lenses Meet the Phoropter

The differences between the trait scale and the growth lens are highlighted by the Phoropter analogy. When you sit behind the Phoropter, its primary lens pair stays put so that you're looking through them at all times, and the secondary lenses swivel behind the primary pair, layered against them. In other words, the primary lenses always affect what you see when you use a Phoropter.

Interpretive Lenses in the Trait Scale

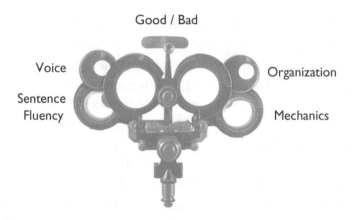

Good / Bad

Voice

Organization

Sentence
Fluency

Mechanics

When we use the trait scale to interpret writing, the good–bad binary is always positioned as the primary lens pair. Every textual trait we examine, from voice to organization, must be seen through this binary and judged accordingly. That's relatively straightforward for something like mechanics, where there's a generally accepted sense of right and wrong (although the more you know about linguistics, the more you realize it's not quite that straightforward). However, looking at writing through the good–bad binary devastates our ability to understand and describe something as complex as organization or voice.

To try to make our trait scale Phoropter work better for us, we can make several modifications. We can add, delete, or swap out the secondary lenses: we might throw in Originality and take out Sentence Fluency. We can also euphemize the title of our primary lens, changing Bad to Not Yet Effective to make it sound less judge-y. We can attach numbers or descriptors to the good–bad continuum or take them out. But no matter what modifications we make, the basic design of the trait scale remains the same; that binary will never be dislodged as the primary lens pair. The limitations resulting from this design, then, can never be overcome. The trait scale (and any tool it is embedded within) will always produce unidimensional judgments and miss complexities that don't fit neatly on that scale.

As the Phoropter reminds us, the lenses we look through influence what we see. So, it's optically naive to insist that we can use the trait scale to produce the grade but comment in our own way. The trait scale changes what we see, and thus influences how we comment. This isn't a theoretical point: large-scale research notes the ways in which most teacher commentary is written to justify the grade (see, for example, Daiker 1989; Connors and Lunsford 1993).

When we use the story and growth lenses to interpret writing, however, decision making is our primary lens pair. That's because we cannot learn to write by following orders. That might work for memorizing multiplication tables. But to compose, we have to make an endless string of decisions. And there's never one right decision; you're deciding between dozens of plausible decisions every decision you make. In addition to reflecting the reality of composing, our decision-making lens supports our larger goal of preparing students to write in a more inclusive and equal democracy.

Interpretive Lenses in Assessment for Growth

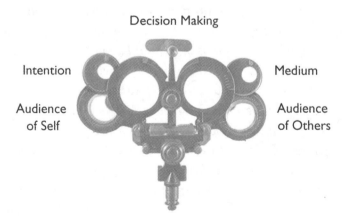

Decision Making

Intention

Medium

Audience of Self

Audience of Others

The primacy of the decision-making lens in our growth Phoropter changes what we're looking at when we assess. The good–bad binary brings the text itself or various textual features or traits into focus. (It's possible to look at the writer through the good–bad binary, but most enlightened teachers are rightfully squeamish about calling students "good" or "bad" writers, at least publicly. It works against a growth mind-set, for one thing.) The growth lenses, however, bring the writer into view. After all, its primary lens pair, decision making, implies and requires a decision maker. We can certainly look at the text itself, but the text comes into view through our growth lenses as an artifact of the decisions the writer has made. This changes the focus, goals, and activities of assessment considerably.

Assessing for Decision Making: "What Are You Thinking?"

The point of looking through the decision-making lens isn't to pronounce a writer's decision-making process good or bad. After all, the good–bad binary doesn't show up in our growth lenses at all. The point of assessing for decision making is to figure out *how* the writer is making decisions. In the process of our inquiry, we might come to judgment, but these judgments don't need to be unidimensional. For example, in "What Are You Thinking?" Katie Wood Ray comes to judgment during a conversation with a fourth-grade writer:

> I asked the first student I met with (who had written about four sentences) to tell me why she had decided to start her letter in the particular way that she did. "What were you thinking?" I asked. As one of the observing teachers noted, the young girl looked at me as though she had just had a frontal lobotomy. All my wonderful wait time provided no answer. I finally realized it was because there wasn't any answer. The student hadn't been asked to do any THINKING or decision-making at all. The topic had been assigned, a graphic organizer told her exactly what to include in each part, and when I sat down next to her, she was simply transferring information from the organizer to a worksheet on which she was supposed to write the letter. The point is, it's difficult for students to answer questions about their thinking when the work they are doing doesn't require them to think. (2006, 59)

"What Are You Thinking?" is an article about pedagogy, not assessment. Still, we can see the story tool working together with the growth lenses in this passage. Katie Wood Ray looks briefly at the text itself (four sentences), but she's more interested in the author's motivations for writing it. This demonstrates a concern with all the things that stories can illuminate: the motivations and actions of the writer as well as the context of the writing. As Ray interprets this story, she focuses on decision making, the most basic of our growth lenses.

After realizing that the student doesn't seem to be making many decisions of her own, Katie Wood Ray comes to a judgment. But she doesn't judge the student a bad decision maker. Instead, she judges the assignment miseducative. Although she doesn't use the word *miseducative*, we can use Dewey's philosophy of experience to frame her observations: the assignment leads the student to experience writing as direction following rather than writing as decision making. Therefore, it leads to growth in the wrong direction.

What can a teacher do with this assessment? Everything. It presents a new, productive problem to be solved. To grow in the right direction, the student needs to be actively involved in the decisions that constitute the act of writing. Therefore, the teacher needs to figure out how to design a writing experience in which the student's decision-making faculties are fully invested. Designing these sorts of experiences takes all our skill as teachers, but it's also what's so interesting about teaching. Like composing, teaching is a creative, expressive, social act, and you can't learn to teach by following orders. Like composing, teaching requires the teacher to be an active decision maker, working within a particular context and informed by her intentions, her relationship with her audience (students), and her relationship with the subject matter and methods. But that's another book.

Ray published "What Are You Thinking?" over ten years ago, underscoring an assertion I made in the last chapter: the assessment practices I'm describing in this book are nothing new. What's new is the claim that *this is assessment*: that it has theoretical and ideological foundations that need to be articulated; that it can't very well coexist with traditional trait scale-based assessment (which perpetuates its own sociopolitical-educational system); and that it has a better chance of forming healthy writers and furthering the cause of a more inclusive and equitable democracy. (Surely we'd want young writers in a democracy to practice their decision-making skills early?)

If this isn't assessment, then I'm hanging up my assessment jersey. It's the only kind of assessment that interests me. Yes, I submit grades at the end of each semester, and theoretically, these grades should have something to do with assessment. And yes, every semester I'm required to enter my ratings of student work to the online database that my college has purchased at great expense in hopes of being accredited by the Council for the Accreditation of Educator Preparation. These ratings are generated by a common rubric that the faculty created the year before I was hired.

I've been teaching in the real world for the past twenty years, and I know that these institutional commitments are very real and very pressing. I sometimes make compromises in light of them. But unless I put these commitments to the side, I cannot get clear about my intentions. And if I can't get clear about my intentions, especially when everything around me is working against them, it's difficult to imagine, much less practice, assessment that supports writers and affirms my best instincts as a teacher and citizen.

Assessing for Intentions: "Feeling, Impulse, Meaning, and Intention"

When I use the story tool and growth lenses, I try to get a sense of the writer's intentions. Immediately. Before I start reading. *Definitely* before I start talking. That's because intention puts in motion and influences all the decisions that constitute the act of writing. In *Everyone Can Write*, Peter Elbow describes the process of writing for veteran and novice writers alike:

> *Most writers engage in a process that students too can participate in: starting with incomplete pieces of feeling, impulse, meaning, and intention—and gradually building them into completed texts; letting the process of writing itself lead them to idea and structures they hadn't planned at the start. (2000, 363)*

Of course, Elbow describes how it's supposed to be. As Katie Wood Ray's story illustrates, school writing often systematically strips away the student's intention to the point where students don't know that they're supposed to have intentions at all. Setting the purpose for writing at the top of the writing assignment sheet isn't the same thing as saying that the student is finding and developing her intentions. A few students can internalize these preset purposes and do a pretty good job of making them their own, but this doesn't happen for most students, and internalizing an external purpose isn't necessarily the same thing as coming to your own intentions. Yes, perhaps writers need to be able to do both. But it's difficult to tell a writer who has never experienced writing from her own intentions that she should take the externally set purpose and act as if it's her own. For writers to grow, they need lots of practice finding and developing their intentions and using them to make decisions as they write.

In my experience, the older a student is, the more distant her intentions become from the writing she produces for school. You'll recall that Bob and Jonah's intentions were fully alive as they composed. I didn't have to worry about whether or not they *had* intentions. They were oozing with intention. When I teach adolescent and adult writers, I usually have to worry. It's not that they don't have intentions; it's that they've learned to separate their intentions from the writing they're required to do for school. I have taught writing in middle school, high school, adult education, community college, and the university. I find that half the work is convincing students that their intentions matter and that they will have time, freedom, guidance, and support in my class to develop them.

Assessing for Intention: Conversation Starters

- Tell me what you're working on and how it's going.
- How did you get the idea for this?
- What made you write about this?
- What are you trying to do here?
- How did you start this?
- How are you feeling about this?

continues

- What were you thinking when you wrote this?
- Is there anything that's not here that you really wanted to be here?
- Does this do you what you want it to do?
- Tell me what it was like when you were working on this.
- Did your ideas or feelings about this essay change while you were working on it?

Assessment for me, then, starts with questions about a student's intentions. Some of these questions are very indirect. They don't use the word *intention*, but they usually get us there in a roundabout way. I've learned from experience that these conversations about intention need to happen early and often. So I generally meet with students before they begin writing, or when they're partway through a draft. These "idea conferences"—whether they're held outside of class, or in class while students are working—often take predictable paths. I've represented one of these paths below. It's not an actual transcript, but an amalgam of hundreds of similar conversations I've had. This comes from a course I'm currently teaching for first-year students in our secondary education program. The assignment is to investigate (through any form or genre) the concept of perspective taking, which will frame all the theories and practices we will explore during the course. But the real assignment is for students to find and develop their own intentions for the assignment.

Maja: So, tell me what you're working on and how it's going.

Student: Well, I have a draft here. Do you want to read it?

Maja: Sure, I'm happy to read it, but I want you to tell me about it, first. How are you feeling about it?

Student: It's OK, I guess. I think it's what we're supposed to be doing.

Maja: What were you trying to do?

Student: Ummm, I don't know. I guess I was trying to do the assignment.

Maja: Are you happy with what you're writing about?

Student: I guess it fits the assignment.

Maja: But I want you to be writing about what you want to write about. *That's* the assignment. Are you writing about what you want to be writing about?

Student: Seriously, what I want? That's a weird question. Maybe not so much.

Maja: So, let's go back to the beginning. I only have two goals for this assignment. I want you to explore perspective taking, because that's a key concept in our course; everything's going to build on it, so I want the concept to be integrated into your own experience, and writing about it is a great way to do that. But my other goal is for you to write about something that feels important to you. So, we've talked a lot about perspective taking in class. Why don't you tell me what comes to mind when you think about perspective taking?

Student: (Starts to tell stories, and gets really animated while telling the fifth story, about how the student's brother temporarily lost the ability to speak in an accident. The brother was becoming agitated in the hospital every time a family member asked him a question, until the student started talking to his injured brother about how confused and frustrated he must feel. The student gave his brother permission to take his time getting better; the family would wait until he was ready to speak. The brother calmed down.)

Maja: I noticed that you got really into that last story—you even did that thing that people do while losing themselves in a story, where they start talking about something that happened a long time ago in present tense like it's happening right now. In fact, you said one line that really stood out to me, "It was like I was inside his head." That strikes me as an interesting first line. Would you want to write about that?

Student: You mean, I can do that? I hadn't thought about that before.

Maja: Well, it's a perfect illustration of perspective taking, and you sound really into it.

Student: Yeah, that's a lot better than what I have here.

Maja: Well, I'm still happy to read it if you want—you already put some work into it.

Student: No, you don't need to read it. I just wrote something down because I was supposed to bring a draft. This idea is a lot better.

Once again, *this* is assessment. The student is in a much better position to write when his intention is at least involved in the topic or idea for the writing. But that's just the start.

"But My Dad's Not a Bad Guy!": Miranda's Dilemma

Once a writer's intentions are invested in the topic, that doesn't mean that the choices she makes from then on will express her intentions in the way that she wants. That's what makes writing difficult, and it's also what makes it so important *not* to give suggestions and feedback without hearing first from the writer. This was a lesson I learned from Miranda.

Miranda was a student in my eleventh-grade writing class at Ludington High School, where I taught a two-course writing sequence in the college-prep track. The eleventh-grade class began with personal narratives and moved into informational writing, and the twelfth-grade class focused on researched argumentative writing. Miranda came to my eleventh-grade class very anxious about writing. She was a successful student and a successful athlete (as a junior, she was the basketball team captain and high scorer). She worried that my class would ruin her grade point average. She considered herself a "math and science person," definitely "not a writer." Part of what she liked about math and science, she told me at the beginning of the semester, was that there were clear-cut right answers. In English, she said, the answers weren't clear and she was therefore unsure how to get a good grade.

From these early conversations, I knew I wanted to help Miranda shift from a performance focus to a content focus; worry about external achievements might very well use up the energy she needed to devote to finding and developing her own intentions. For the first several weeks of class, we did lots of low-stakes writing activities and journal entries aimed at finding something with a little bit of fire behind it to develop into a longer piece. I was pleased to see that Miranda found a topic through these activities that she was genuinely excited to explore: how her relationship with her dad had unfolded through their shared love of basketball.

When students submitted their first drafts, I asked them to write me a note describing how they felt about what they'd written, how the writing had gone, and if there was anything specific they wanted me to comment on. I read Miranda's draft before I read her note to me. In fact, it was Miranda's paper that would convince me to listen to how the students felt about their drafts before reading the draft itself. Here's Miranda's first draft:

The New Hoop
By Miranda

Cameron was standing atop the ladder; ball in hand. He glanced nervously at my dad who was beaming right at his side. The three of us had just put up the new hoop outside our house since I had dunked one too many times on the other one and the pole bent. Dad gave Cam the thumbs up so Cameron laid the basketball right over the rim and it swished through the net hitting the ground with a thud. I smiled to myself a few feet behind him and helped him down from the ladder. It seemed like just yesterday I was the one laying the ball over the rim on our old hoop.

Dad and I spent hours on end in the gym and now I needed a hoop outside of my own to play on since I always wanted to be shooting. Basketball has always been the connection between my dad and I. We tend to clash on almost all other subjects, friends, boyfriends, homework, work time management, and cell phone bills. All our differences seem to disappear on the court though.

When I was in 4th grade my family moved to a different house on the other side of town and there was no hoop. So, of course, as soon as we moved in my dad and I tried to find the best spot in our new driveway to put a basketball hoop. We measured lengths and widths of 10 different spots to make sure we picked the spot with the most space. I loved every minute we spent out in the driveway, yelling out numbers while he'd write them down, and direct me to the next spot. Then Dad and I spent two days straight constructing the hoop in the garage. I love putting things together, I was always doing puzzles and Lego sets so this was right down my alley. There was actually one part my dad did wrong and I remember him shaking his head and smiling when I corrected him. Dad would always let me attempt to screw in all the nuts and bolts, but I could never quite get them all the way so he'd always finish up for me. He never made me feel scrawny for not being strong enough. After a few hours of building in the garage the hoop was all put together and just needed to be cemented into the ground. As we mixed the cement and poured it in the hole with the pole of the hoop being held straight up, it was like my dad and I were cementing our relationship through basketball also. The cement had been left to dry for two whole days, but finally Dad came and told me it was okay to play now. He also said I got to shoot the first basket. I was instantly ecstatic; after all this work on the hoop and he was going to let me shoot first. Then he told me, "You know, you have to make the first shot or else the hoop will be bad luck."

Boy did that get me nervous. Luckily, as I walked outside I saw a ladder placed right under the hoop. I breathed a huge sigh of relief. Dad was going to make sure I didn't miss. That's how he's always been, making sure I'm still shooting straight. He makes sure I do what's right, even if I think he's taking it too far sometimes. I realize now he just wants what's best for me, and I know now that most of the time (as much as I hate to admit it) he's right. As I reached for the top of the ladder I looked down at my dad and he smiled wide and handed me the ball. He always has given me all the tools I've ever needed to make sure I succeed at whatever I want to. He'll put his life on hold just to make sure I'm all right and can get the things I need to get me where I want to go in life.

*Now that I'm older and making more of my own decisions
I don't always want to "take the ball from my dad" I want
to go get it myself. Some nights when I'll be outside shooting
around a little bit my dad will come outside and try to make
conversation about my future in basketball. "how much time
have you spent outside shooting this week?" he'll ask.*

*"I don't know, maybe 2 hours I guess." Exaggerating
because I know he'd be disappointed if he knew the real
amount.*

*"You need more arc on your shot, you're throwing it
again." I feel my jaw clench and my temper rise. Here we go
again, I think to myself. He starts up again on the lecture I
already have memorized, "You know if you're going to get
better you need to be working more, and concentrate on the
little things.*

*Sometimes he pushed too far, it almost seems like he
wants me to be the same way he was, and I need to be my
own person. My dad made the mistake of not playing college
basketball when he had the opportunity to, and I wonder
now if he pushes me so hard to play because he thinks I
might make the same mistake for myself. He tries to act all
right with my uncertainty about college ball, but I know it
kills him to hear me question how much I want it. He wants
basketball to be my own passion in life, and sometimes I'm
not 100% sure that's what's in the cards for me. I know my
dad loves me and only wants what's best for me, but what I
do with my future is my decision and I'm prepared to make
that decision for myself.*

Given Miranda's reservations about writing, I was delighted. In
class, we'd worked on writing scenes to convey meaning without
hitting your reader over the head with *the moral of the story.* I could
picture all of Miranda's scenes, and although each was interesting in its
own right, they were more than the sum of their parts. Together, they
created the tension that animated the essay.

Most importantly, though, Miranda was using writing to grapple
with important issues in her life. I suspected that the same anxiety that

Miranda had expressed to me about writing was wrapped up in the conflict she was exploring in her essay: the pressure to live up to someone else's expectations (perhaps to fulfill their unfulfilled dreams?) versus the desire to make her own decisions. Her declaration at the end ("I'm prepared to make that decision for myself") was a strong ending to her classic yet particular coming-of-age story, written just moments before coming-of-age actually arrives.

In fact, Miranda's essay met all my goals for this first draft of the year. She had invested her intentions in exploring something meaningful through writing; from previous conversations and bits of the draft I'd already seen, she had discovered something new through writing it; and she'd clearly tried out some of the writing techniques we'd explored in class. I thought she'd enjoyed writing this essay and could be proud of it, not for the grade she'd earn, but for the way she'd expressed a complex relationship and dilemma in her life. I wasn't even worried about the sports cliché ("making sure I'm still shooting straight"). This was how Miranda talked, and it had its own charm. Plus, have you ever watched a sporting event where the commentator doesn't wipe the court clean with clichés? There was something fitting about it.

I was ready to tell Miranda what I liked about her draft, help her clean up a few issues, and call it a day. Then I read Miranda's note. She was worried that her essay portrayed her dad as a "bad guy" in a way that she didn't intend. This wasn't a passing worry. It consumed her entire note. Miranda's dilemma prompted a dilemma of my own. I was tempted to interpret her worry as a kind of backpedaling, a sign that she was uncomfortable with the developmental progress she was making. I was strongly tempted to say, "But this essay is so great the way it is! Don't back down! You're confronting a dynamic that's important to confront!" In fact, I did say this (or, a version of it, anyway), in a written response that I ultimately erased. At the time, I couldn't quite articulate why I erased it, except that I thought it felt vaguely intrusive.

Looking back, I can see that I would have been using praise to bully Miranda into writing the essay *I* wanted her to write. In fact, I suspected that she was vulnerable to praise in a way that worked against her own interests; that's partly why I was excited by her closing line that proclaimed her readiness to make her own decisions. Yet, I was close to using this vulnerability against Miranda by telling her that her essay was so good that she shouldn't worry about the fact that it didn't match her intentions. It's hypocritical, I know: *She's not going to play college ball just because her dad wants her to, but darn it all if she isn't going keep her essay as is because I want her to!*

In the end, I wrote Miranda a different response:

> *Miranda,*
>
> *You mention your discomfort with the ending. Let's think about it this way: right now, your paper starts with a wonderfully positive memory (building the hoop with your father) and then ends with a more conflicted memory. In other words, the last thing left in the reader's mouth is a "bad taste"—though that is overstating. What if you switch it around so that you start with the conflicted memory, and use the positive memory to help you understand where all this is coming from? That way, the "taste" left in your reader's mouth is a good one, and you've used the positive memory to help you understand a phenomenon that just about every father and daughter go through . . . think this idea through and try it if it seems like it would accomplish what you want.*
>
> *Maja*

Miranda's revision begins with this tension-filled paragraph:

The New Hoop, Draft 2
By *Miranda*

"You need more arc on your shot, you're throwing it again."
I feel my jaw clench and my temper rise. Here we go again,
I think to myself. He starts up again on the lecture I already
have memorized, "you know if you're going to get better you
need to be working more, and concentrate on the little things."

Then, she describes the conflict between her dad's hopes for her and her own before moving into the first flashback, as she and her brother set up the new hoop with her dad supervising. This prompts another flashback, as she and her dad build the new hoop at the new house. Then, the first shot at the new hoop: everything rests on it, but her dad isn't going to let her miss it. Finally, Miranda ties these scenes together with this understanding of her dad's role in her future decisions:

> He'll put his life on hold just to make sure I'm all right and
> can get the things I need to get me where I want to go in life.
> With him behind me and because I had him to help me grow
> I know I'll be able to get wherever it is I want to go.

I considered this second draft equally delightful. The tension is still there, but Miranda negotiates it into a new understanding of her father's role in her life. She wants to be independent, but she can recognize the role that her dad has played in making her strong and capable enough to make decisions on her own. After all, her dad's influence and support will get her "wherever it is I want to go." She's renegotiated the conflict, and she hasn't given anything up in the process.

Has there been growth? If we ask the trait scale, no. The essays are organized differently, but equally well. There are a few more mechanical errors in the first draft, but probably not enough to move from one rating for conventions to another. Otherwise, in terms of sentence fluency or voice, they're no different; it's mostly the same writing as the first draft, but reorganized. If we subtract the rating of the first draft from the rating of the second draft, then, we come up with a grand difference of 0. The trait scale doesn't reveal growth between these drafts.

If we use our growth lenses, however, we're not just looking at the drafts and asking whether they're good or bad and which one is better. We're looking at Miranda and her relationship to her intentions as she wrote the drafts. And we're asking whether the experience of writing one draft after another, with our conversation in between, led to growth in the right direction. If I'd succeeded in convincing Miranda that her first draft was so great that she should just polish it up a little, the experience might have been agreeable enough. Who doesn't like praise? Who doesn't like less work?

However, this advice would have been miseducative in at least one important way. Miranda would have learned that her intentions matter less than the teacher's, even a teacher who says she cares about her intentions. Miranda's grade point average would have held strong, but her relationship with her intentions would have remained distant, if not fractured further. Surely, some teachers will assert that Miranda needs to be responsive to her readers' preferences and might see nothing wrong with overwriting her intentions with their own suggestions. But when we're teaching healthy writers who write within (and for) a more inclusive and equitable democracy, we have to take seriously the constant tension in a democracy between the interests of the individual and the interests of the group. We can't glibly dismiss either side.

In fact, I'd already made an assessment of this tension between individual and others in Miranda's development as a writer before working with her on "The New Hoop." I'd decided that Miranda's relationship with writing had suffered because she viewed writing as a reflection of her status within the community, not as a tool to understand herself and her relationship with others, the world, and ideas. This assessment led to my goal for working with Miranda: to encourage Miranda to forget about the grade and to focus instead on what she was trying to say and how her text reflected her intent. My position on the role of Miranda's intentions, then, was negotiated within the larger context of self in society and was informed by my understanding of intrinsic motivation. This kind of nuance opens up when we stop using assessment to rank students' abilities.

But we aren't quite ready to judge if Miranda's second draft represents growth in the right direction. To determine that, we have to understand how Miranda felt about her second draft, and how she experienced the process of writing it. Here's an excerpt from her end-of-course reflection:

> *I was a lot happier with the new ending and how our*
> *relationship was depicted . . . it really grasped my*
> *relationship with my dad and made me realize some things*
> *in the process . . . I am finally looking for way to better the*
> *actual content . . . your feedback helped me because you*

didn't force your opinion on me, and helped bring out my discontent with my writing and fix it.

When we look at Miranda through a double layer of lenses—decision making and intention—we see that Miranda has found a way to make her words better align with her intentions. And this experience gives her a new way to look at future writing ("I am finally looking for a way to better the actual content"). No matter how any "blind rater" would rank Miranda's drafts, this is what Dewey meant by growth in the right direction. And it's what I mean by assessment for growth.

6

Voices That Help and Haunt Us

The Enabling, Paralyzing Paradox of Audience

Sometimes we write to express ourselves to no one in particular, like singing with the stereo cranked up so that not even you can hear you. Sometimes we write to connect with readers, to share with others what we know and feel and wonder and wish. Our audiences can shape our intentions and suggest everything from subject matter and genre to word choice and what happens next, like when Bob ignited and then doused Noah. Sometimes, we solicit our audience's experience so we can know whether our words carry the weight of our meaning, like when Jonah asked, "What does it look like to you?" Sometimes we shift from writer to reader in an instant and determine for ourselves whether what we've written makes sense, like when Jonah proclaimed, "This doesn't look like a porcupine. It looks like a flashlight." And sometimes, a chorus of internalized voices weighs in on what we want to write, how we should write it, and the merits of what we've written.

It's time to look through our decision-making lens at a writer's relationship with an audience of self and others. The goal isn't to judge this relationship as good or bad, but to understand it and to help the writer use it for her own purposes. First, we'll explore some of the complexities of using audience to make decisions. Then, we'll consider the kind of feedback that readers can give writers to support their relationship to their audiences. Finally, we'll combine one writer's intention (Betsy's) with one audience member's experience (mine) to negotiate a revision.

The Voices in Our Head: Self and Others

Vygotsky (1986) believed that thought and language merge around the age of three, as social speech becomes internalized as "inner speech." As Oliver Sacks describes it, inner speech is critical to both consciousness and identity.

> Our real language, our real identity, lies in inner speech,
> in that ceaseless stream and generation of meaning that
> constitutes the individual mind. It is through inner speech
> that the child develops his own concepts and meanings; it
> is through inner speech that he achieves his own identity; it
> is through inner speech, finally, that he constructs his own
> world. (1989, 73)

Scholars debate whether the social or the private uses of speech come first (Jones 2009) or whether this inner voice is abbreviated in the way that Vygotsky claimed it was. But few doubt the experience.

While this inner voice is a running monologue for Vygotsky, it's a dialogue between two distinct selves for Donald Murray. In "Teaching the Other Self: The Writer's First Reader," Murray (1982) describes how these two selves converse in the act of writing. There's the "first self" who writes. Then, there's the "other self" who reads, counsels, and navigates the territory mapped out by the first self. Here's Murray on this inner dialogue:

> *The act of writing might be described as a conversation between two workmen muttering to each other at the workbench. The self speaks, the other self listens and responds. The self proposes, the other self considers. The self makes, the other self evaluates. The two selves collaborate: a problem is spotted, discussed, defined; solutions are proposed, rejected, suggested, attempted, tested, discarded, accepted. (1982, 140)*

Murray argues that the other self gains strength and skill through speaking out loud. The purpose of a writing conference, then, isn't for the teacher to give advice about the writing, but to invite the student's other self to speak—and then to listen. The writer may forget any particular suggestion from the teacher when the class is over. But she'll always take her other self with her. It's the *person* who grows, after all. Or, to add Murray's twist, it's the *selves* and *their voices* that grow, after all.

This may seem like a lot of voices and selves. In my experience, however, it's just the start of the bedlam. After all, not all of voices in my head are my own. Every time I eat a piece of cantaloupe, for instance, I hear my father saying, "Maja, you can't elope!" I'm five states and several decades away from the last time he actually said this, but it still sounds exactly like him: fully committed to the pun and as delighted the 1,000th time he's said it as the first.

This phenomenon I recognize as my father's voice isn't just a memory of things he's said in the past. It's more like a perspective that I attribute to him, capable of generating novel statements in response to novel situations. I know that I'm imagining some of these statements, using what I know of my dad's principles and preferences to anticipate his reactions. But this voice doesn't quite feel like me, either. It feels like a collaboration. Sometimes I talk back, and sometimes it converses with other voices I've also internalized or even flat-out made up. These voices often get louder when I write, and I've had to learn to work with (and sometimes against) them.

The point is: when we consider the relationship between a writer and an audience of self and others, it's more complex than simply saying, "We write for ourselves" or, "We write for readers." A veritable chorus of voices may be involved—real, conjured, and completely fabricated—and the line between self and other may sometimes blur. Whether literal or figurative, whether ours or theirs (or both), these voices influence our intentions, make suggestions, and second-guess or even veto decisions. When we use the lenses of audience of self and others to understand how a writer makes decisions, then, we're not just considering the audience listed on the assignment sheet that the student is supposed to be writing for. We're looking at the writer's relationship to all the voices in her head.

Contentious Relationships: Managing the Unproductive Voices

These voices aren't always helpful. In *Bird by Bird*, Anne Lamott (1994) dramatizes her vexed relationship with the voices inside her head. At the start of any writing project, they nag, judge, whine, and make demands—sometimes paralyzing her. On the advice of a hypnotist, she isolates each voice, imagines it as a mouse, picks it up by the tail, drops it into a glass jar with a volume control button, screws the lid shut, and turns up the volume all the way. Then she turns the volume down and watches the mice silently claw at the glass before setting the jar aside so that she can return, in peace, to writing her "shitty first draft" (21).

Peter Elbow (1987) makes the point less dramatically but no less powerfully in "Closing My Eyes as I Speak: An Argument for Ignoring Audience." He explains that he often closes his eyes when struggling to articulate an idea in front of a live audience (50). It's not that his audience nags or whines like the voices in Anne Lamott's head. Instead, their very presence distracts Elbow from his thoughts.

I've seen Elbow close his eyes while speaking. He describes this move as potentially impolite or even antisocial, but I've found that it has the effect of conveying the seriousness with which he is taking a particular encounter. Even though he's been thinking about these issues for his entire career, this is a unique moment—in part because you're in it—and a unique moment demands a unique utterance.

Sometimes, he's got to block you out to give you and his idea the thoughtfulness you both deserve.

It can be tempting at this point to ask, "Wait, are you saying that thinking about audience is bad? Should we all write like William Burroughs, wrapped up in our own heads, and if no one else can understand what we write, it's because they just aren't groovy enough to dig it?" Half a century ago I might have said yes. But now I know that this question misses the point. It's those pesky binary assessment lenses again, which always make us choose: *is thinking about audience good or bad?* But if we can observe and describe the writer's relationship with audience in all its contradiction and complexity, then we can figure out what the writer wants and needs. Then we can decide what to do about it. That's essentially what Anne Lamott is doing with the jar metaphor. She pays attention to each voice for a moment, acknowledges the effect it has on her, then she puts the voices aside because she'd rather write.

Of course, writers won't always want to silence the voices. Consider Bob's relationship with his real-life audience, Noah. Noah's voice is generative for Bob; his presence shapes Bob's intentions from start to finish. Provoking and then appeasing Noah is the subject, process, and final form of Bob's composition.

We're left, then, with a paradox. Thinking about audience isn't good *or* bad. It's good *and* bad. Like all paradoxes, the surface contradiction maintains a deeper unity. In this case, the unity is revealed when we consider a writer's relationship with audience through the lens of intention. Thinking about audience is *good* when it helps you develop and clarify your intentions, and thinking about audience is *bad* when it takes you further from your intentions. In this way, the paradox preserves complexity. And this complexity is embedded in the revolving, layered lenses of our growth Phoropter.

Collaborative Relationships: Voices Worthy of Internalizing

I've always wondered if any of the critical mice in Anne Lamott's glass jar represent the voices of English teachers past. I hope not, but there's reason to worry. After all, when I tell strangers what I do for a living, they are sure to blush, assert that they can't spell or are terrible at grammar, and then they avoid me. I certainly haven't commented on their spelling or grammar, but my very presence apparently conjures up corrections and judgments from days of yore.

It's not that we English teachers are terrible people to haunt our students in this way. We've been beholden to those judgmental assessment lenses and the scales that reify them. Whether criticism and judgment are naturally part of an English teacher's personality or perspective, these binary lenses have contributed to our message and tone as we interact with students as they write. Dewey (1938) asserted that every experience lives on in future experiences. We could say the same about voices. Will our voices someday need to be exorcised?

I once asked my ninth-grade students if they heard their own voice when they read silently to themselves. One particularly avid young reader explained that his third-grade teacher had read aloud to the class every day after lunch, and she always created different voices for different characters. Six years later, he still heard this third-grade teacher's voice in his head when he read. Others in the class also fondly remembered this teacher. Reading would be a better experience, one student commented, if this teacher had actually followed him to high school to read everything aloud to him.

If students can find the echo of our voices helpful as they read to themselves, perhaps they could use our voices as they write, too. What would we say now if we wanted our voices to actually help students in the future? It isn't that I *want* my voice echoing in a student's head years later. In fact, I'm slightly disturbed by the idea. But it's bound to happen sometimes—that's just the way that we affect each other—and I'd rather my voice encourage and ask productive questions than make someone cringe and shy away from writing. So, if a student conjures up my voice in all, I'd want it to emphatically remind her that it's her intentions and voice that matter the most. That's why my questions and feedback are not shaped by standards or learning targets. Instead, my voice is shaped first by my understanding of how writing works and how writers develop. These understandings are embedded in the growth lenses of decision making, intention, audience of self and others, and medium.

In other words, without sacrificing individuality, we can use the growth lenses as principles to shape what we say and how we say it. The intention lens is particularly important to me, especially because school writing so consistently ignores students' intentions. However, I know that a writer's intentions are often shaped by her relationship with audience (self and others, real and imagined), not to mention her relationship with the medium (written words and genre). These considerations often overlap in practice. By allowing my questions and response to be influenced by the growth lenses, I'm hoping that students will collaborate with my English teacher voice as it lives on in students' future writing experiences.

Reimagining Our Expertise: The Newcomer and Beginner Within

When I moved to rural Maine, I was simultaneously amused and frustrated by the directions I'd get from strangers: "You'll want to turn left where the old Dairy Queen used to be before it burned down." That's a perfect direction for someone who was born here and remembers the old Dairy Queen. It's a terrible direction for a newcomer.

As readers of our own writing, we were born here; we can easily project all our intended meanings onto our words. That's fine if we're writing for ourselves. But when we want to convey those meanings to an audience of others, it can take a newcomer to remind us of the gap between what's on the page and what's still hidden in our own experience. It's possible to internalize the newcomer's perspective, shifting back and forth within ourselves between writer and reader like Murray's muttering workmen. But we can't internalize a reader's voice we've never heard.

In other words, writers need readers who will describe their experience of their words as honestly and carefully as possible. Notice, that's a different proposition than, "Writers need readers who will compare their writing to an ideal or standard—as a whole, or criterion by criterion." That's not a superficial difference between a judgment and an *I* statement, like the difference between saying, "This is bad" and, "I feel that this is bad." As Peter Elbow (1973) points out, when we assert that the problem with a text is the presence or absence of a particular feature ("Too much detail!"), we're making an hypothesis or abstract theory about how writing works. However, when we describe the text's effect on us, we're stating an empirical fact ("About two pages into the details about your eccentric neighbor I got really into picturing this crazy character with his little yapping dogs and argyle sweaters, but then I remembered that your profile is about your dad, and I did start wondering if your profile is really more about your neighbor").

In several important ways, English teachers are the perfect people to offer descriptions of our experience of reading students' texts. We're good at thinking carefully about the effects of words, and we're generally good at description. In other important ways, however, our expertise and training work against us. Part of that training involves our knowledge of formats and rules: "The thesis should go at the end of the introduction." This format-based rule contains no reference to a reader's experience at all: in fact, you don't actually have to read an entire essay to know if a student has followed this rule. If we think of assessment and evaluation as comparing a student's work to a standard, rule, format, or other abstraction, then, we're less likely to embody the perspective of a newcomer as we read. And we're less likely to communicate to young writers how the exchange between writer, reader, and text actually works.

What I've been calling the newcomer's perspective is reminiscent of Shoshin, a concept in Zen Buddhism commonly referred to as "beginner's mind." Beginner's mind is a state in which experts and nonexperts alike encounter a subject without preconceptions or the labels and categories of the expert. Consider how these first graders bring their beginner's minds to the ellipsis. In "What Are You Thinking?" Katie Wood Ray (2006) shares an exchange in which teacher Lisa Cleveland asks her first-grade class what they're thinking about an ellipsis and how they'd use it as a writer. After the initial question, the class is off on this romp of a discussion.

> **CAROLINA:** You could use it like a surprise party. Like you're hiding under a table and then you put a little ellipsis and you say, "Surprise!"

TEACHER: So what would your words be *before* the ellipsis? What would you be saying?

CAROLINA: "One . . . two . . . three . . . " [her voice rises after each number, indicating the placement of the ellipsis].

TEACHER: I hear it! Did you hear it in her voice? "One . . . two . . . three . . . " and then we turn the page and what do you have?

EVERYONE: Surprise!

[More conversation.]

ANNA: It's like a guy hanging off a cliff and then everything freezes.

TEACHER: Because that ellipsis is leaving you hanging there, like, "What's going to come next?"

ANNA: Yeah. Like he's thinking, "Am I going to fall or stay on the cliff?" (2006, 58)

Carolina and Anna don't have the grammarian's tools for describing the proper use and function of a punctuation mark. But they know how an ellipsis makes an audience feel—tense, suspended—because they've found and studied multiple examples and have accumulated these feelings from all those contexts. So instead of reciting the definition or the rule, they fold their experience of the ellipsis into metaphors: "You're hiding under a table" and "A guy hanging off a cliff and then everything freezes." If they wanted their readers to feel that way, they'd use that punctuation mark as a writer. They don't need the grammarian's tools; their beginner's minds are perfectly capable of thinking in terms of intentions, medium, and effects.

We expect this fresh perspective from children because it's *all* new to them. But what about the expert in the room, Lisa Cleveland? It's far too easy (and common) for experts to use their expertise to assert their own authority and defend their disciplinary territory. But that's a deadly move for a teacher, whose job it is to make the discipline not just accessible to the beginner, but also welcoming. In fact, welcoming students into the writer's world is exactly what Cleveland does in this conversation. She doesn't dismiss her students' descriptions of the ellipsis as "cute" or reduce their imaginings and feelings to a single disciplinary term. Instead, she adopts and gives voice to the beginner's mind and constructs the class' understandings around it. The result is powerful, deep understanding.

An Audience That Illuminates: How the Beginner's Mind Can Shape the Story of Our Reading

Assessors rarely approach students' texts with the kind of beginner's mind that Lisa Cleveland brings to her teaching. That's because assessment traditionally involves evaluation or critique, and these activities imply a position of power over the critiqued or the evaluated. And critics and evaluators often derive their position of power from access to exclusive knowledge: criteria that only the critic is knowledgeable enough to construct or apply. When teachers read students' writing to assess it, then, they're likely to adopt a position that is antithetical to the beginner's mind—and thus, to the kind of feedback that writers need to access their audiences' experiences.

Despite its rarity (or perhaps because of it), there is nothing more illuminating than when the critic approaches the criticism with a beginner's mind. Consider Nancy Franklin's 2011 review of *The Killing*. Franklin is an expert critic; she has worked for the *New Yorker* since the 1970s, reviewing theatre and then television. But consider the position she adopts when she opens this review:

> *I haven't been responding to the new AMC drama "The Killing" with the ardency that other critics and civilians I know have shown. Where is my heart, I wondered as I watched the first handful of episodes of the show, a mystery involving the murder of a teen-age girl. Where is my soul? Do I no longer have eyes to see? Do I not have the stomach for this? Is my liver producing too much bile? What's wrong with me?*

This isn't snide criticism in the form of a question. These are actually the questions that drive the review. Instead of asserting an evaluation, Franklin explores her experience ("Watching the show, I felt as though I were in an abusive relationship") and tries to figure out why she's having the reaction she's having ("I'm still figuring it out, but perhaps I've found a clue").

For example, Franklin suggests that a feeling of "I've been here before" may have interfered with her enthusiasm. She points out the echoes of *Twin Peaks* in the show's promotional materials:

> *In the weeks before the series began, ads asking the question "Who Killed Rosie Larsen?" kept cropping up, and it took no effort to discern an echo of the promo line for the David Lynch–Mark Frost series "Twin Peaks"… the atmospherics of that series are an institution now, familiar to any television viewer who's old enough to watch "The Killing."*

Although I was certainly old enough to have seen *Twin Peaks*, I hadn't. Franklin's hypothesis (that she was perhaps less interested in the atmospherics of *The Killing* because she'd seen them before) made me wonder: are plots or atmospherics only interesting if they're original? Would I find *The Killing* less interesting if I had already seen *Twin Peaks*? That question sent me back to Netflix to begin watching *Twin Peaks* alongside *The Killing*. Instead of closing me off to the show, this negative review had sent me further into it than if I'd just discovered it on my own.

The point isn't that *The Killing* is a great or a terrible show, or that Franklin's reaction was right or wrong. The point is that when an expert adopts a beginner's mind and tells the story of her experience, the result is to open up experience rather than close it down. It also makes the process of evaluation more transparent. The great critic Nancy Franklin doesn't sit down to watch a show with a set of criteria to apply to which only she has access. Instead, it appears she sits down to watch a show, has an experience of it, and then tries to figure out what has caused that experience.

If Nancy Franklin can adopt the beginner's mind rather than hiding behind criteria in her evaluation, so can teachers. If we tell the story of our experience of reading, then students are more likely to form useful understandings about how writing and reading work. If students hear our voices in their heads years from now, I hope that our authority comes not from our knowledge and application of criteria, rules, or formats, but from our commitment to the one thing that everyone can engage, describe, and claim: experience.

"This Book Needs You": Movies of the Mind for Assessment

Gary Paulsen begins *The Winter Room* with this startling invocation of experience that functions as a preview to the book's setting and an invitation to the reader:

> *If books could be more, could give more, show more, this book would have sound . . . It would have the chewing sounds of cows in the barn working at their cuds on a long winter's night; the solid thunking sound of the ax coming down to split stovewood, and the piercing scream of the pigs when the knife cuts their throats and they know death is at hand—but it can't. Books can't have sound . . . If books could have more, give more, show more, this book would still need readers, who bring to them sound and smell and light and all the rest that can't be in books. This book needs you. (1989, 2–3)*

Without the experiences of readers, Paulsen reminds us, texts are just pages with little marks on them. Writing assessment ignores Paulsen's insight at the risk of its own undoing. Without readers, we can only evaluate the text by weighing the paper or counting the little marks. Once readers are involved, we can't evaluate a text unless we're also evaluating our experience of reading the text.

As early as 1973, Peter Elbow asserted that readers should narrate their experience of reading to give the writer an honest account of "what happened in *you* when you read the words *this time*" (85). He called this technique "movies of the mind." Here's Elbow and Pat Belanoff's explanation of movies of the mind from *Sharing and Responding*:

> *The story of what goes on in readers is what we need most as writers; not evaluation of the quality of our writing or advice about how to fix it but an accurate account of what our words did to readers. We need to learn to feel those readers*

*on the other end of our line. When are they with us? When
are their minds wandering? What are they thinking and
feeling? What do they hear us saying? (1989)*

Even as I transcribe this quote, I'm feeling a bit silly: if Elbow had
this figured out almost fifty years ago, why am I acting as if this were a
new insight?

It certainly isn't a new insight. But, in my own defense, movies of
the mind has mainly been discussed as a response technique for nonexperts, not an assessment technique for teachers: for democratically
run groups in *Writing Without Teachers* (Elbow 1973) and for peer
revision in *Sharing and Responding* (Elbow and Belanoff 1989). It's true
that movies of the mind is a way of responding to readers. But response
is *based in* assessment. If assessment equals (or even includes) grading,
response will be constructed to justify the grade.

Perhaps Elbow puts movies of the mind in the hands of nonexperts who aren't responsible for grading because he doesn't want the
technique to be corrupted. He knows that grading causes teachers to
ask the wrong questions while they read. When we grade, we're asking
ourselves, *How does this compare?* or *How good is this?* When we do
movies of the mind, on the other hand, we're asking ourselves, *What
am I experiencing: thinking, feeling, wondering, expecting, and hoping?*

However, I'm prepared to claim movies of the mind as an assessment technique for teachers. After all, my entire vision of assessment
rests on extricating assessment from grading or comparison to a
standard. Instead, assessment involves the attempt to understand and
support a writer's relationship with audience. Movies of the mind is an
assessment technique, then, because it provides a window into the way
that audiences work. It opens up the reading process to the student,
thus strengthening her relationship with an audience of self and others. But the technique also helps teachers. When you're comparing a
text to a standard or set of criteria, it's tempting to skim for features,
which is different than reading. In fact, as Tom Newkirk (2005) points
out in *The School Essay Manifesto*, that's why the five-paragraph essay
was invented; you just make sure the right parts are in the right place.
As the practice of paying attention to your experience of your reading,
then, movies of the mind reminds you to actually read.

Elbow and Belanoff (1989) offer transcripts in *Sharing and Responding* of movies of the mind, and each is about a page long. These alone are worth the price of admission for both *Sharing and Responding* and *Writing Without Teachers* (Elbow 1973), two books that every writing teacher should read. But I'll admit it: I don't *ever* write page-long movies of the mind. Most of the time I don't write them at all. In fact, I don't always say them. That's because movies of the mind is, above all, the practice of paying attention to my experience of a text. Although this experience always *informs* my response, it only sometimes *constitutes* my response.

When Movies of the Mind Stay in the Mind: An Outrageous Number of Letters

Betsy was a first-year student at the University of New Hampshire in my First Year Composition course when I was a graduate student. It was the second week of the course, and Betsy had just come to my office to talk about a draft of her literacy autobiography, an exploration of her relationship with reading or writing. We'd read various literacy autobiographies in class and noted differences in topic, tone, and structure: Frederick Douglass' (1845) account of trading bread for letters; Anne-Marie Oomen's (2006) description of being transfixed by the powerful words etched into an outhouse wall; Tom Romano's (2008) story of finding refuge in the keys of a manual typewriter in the wake of his father's death.

When Betsy handed me her draft, I asked how the writing had gone. She wasn't sure. She'd tried her best, but questioned whether what she'd written qualified as a literacy autobiography. The same sentiment was reflected in the draft reflection she'd written:

> *I feel like I'm not really getting my point across. I love writing about OB because it is something I am proud of and I have vivid memories of because it was so hard for me. Is this an appropriate Literacy Autobiography? I tried to add in other stories but they feel a little forced, do you think they add anything or are necisary?*

With Betsy sitting next to me, I read her draft quickly. I'd never worked with Betsy before, so the movies of my mind stayed in my mind. I've found that they can be quite overwhelming for any writer who is used to the praise–criticism dichotomy—which almost all older students are—especially in an early draft where there's probably a lot that doesn't work yet. So when I first start working with a writer, I keep the movie of my mind to myself: it's simply my way of paying attention to how the draft works in me. Combined with my understanding of the writer's intention, this is the foundation for any response I might make.

BETSY'S DRAFT	MOVIES OF THE MIND: MY EXPERIENCE OF BETSY'S DRAFT
Betsy's first paragraph: Cold feet, heavy packs, and unexpected weather, are generally associated with Holderness School's Outback Program (OB). OB is a ten day camping trip in March in which Holderness School juniors have participated in for decades. During the ten days, students hike the White Mountains, participate in a three night solo, and experience group bonding. I was petrified, and had been since the seventh grade, when I began thinking about going to Holderness. The whole idea of being alone, the dark, and hiking was not for me, but I had to do it.	**My experience of Betsy's first paragraph:** *I'm drawn in by those first three phrases. It's a drive-by of outdoor images, and I'm thinking that there's going to be lots of camping in this essay. Maybe suffering, too; all those images are slightly foreboding. At that fourth phrase ("are generally associated with Holderness School's Outback Program") I start to fade. It's formal, like lawyer-ese, and I zone out. By the time I get to "I was petrified," I'm pulled back in a bit, wondering why her reaction is so strong, but I'm only reading with half-attention, waiting for something to grab me.*

continues

BETSY'S DRAFT	MOVIES OF THE MIND: MY EXPERIENCE OF BETSY'S DRAFT
Betsy's second paragraph: I made the decision to go to Holderness, and I knew it was the right one. The only thing holding me back from this wonderful experience was Outback, but I kept being told it was too early to worry about it, so I tried not to, but it was always looming over me. Freshman year came and went with many struggles and successes. Shakespeare in English class was one way to make me feel worthless, but I made it through. I recognized that I struggled with reading comprehension, but did nothing about it. All in all I was loving almost every minute of Holderness.	**My experience of Betsy's second paragraph:** *I'm still only half paying attention, looking for something to pull me in. "Looming" in the second sentence catches my attention, but fades quickly. I'm laughing at the idea of Shakespeare making Betsy feel worthless, not because I'm heartless, but because it's such a common story. I'm wondering exactly how Shakespeare made Betsy feel worthless, but we're onto a struggle with reading comprehension, and soon, Betsy is asserting that she's loving Holderness. I'm trying to figure out whether the essay is about camping, or Shakespeare, or reading comprehension?*
Betsy's third paragraph: Then sophomore year came. This was the first time I ever liked my English teacher. He was a younger guy and my roommate and I connected with him very quickly. I still did not like reading, but I would do it for him. We did a project focusing on our reading as a child. In the beginning of the project I said that I always hated reading, but I thought about it more, and realized at one point in my life I loved reading. I always got read bedtime stories. I remember coming downstairs in the beginning of December each year to a big red wicker basket	**My experience of Betsy's third paragraph:** *I'm intrigued by this English teacher, but I'm confused that Betsy has a roommate. Is Holderness a college? Did Betsy transfer to UNH? Or maybe Holderness is a boarding school? That reading project sounds cool, but I'm distracted trying to figure out what this has to do with camping. At the big red wicker basket full of books, I'm fully in; this is one of the first images that I can actually picture. In fact, I'm wondering if this essay is really about that Christmas morning, not camping? I know I'm supposed to be thinking only about my experience*

BETSY'S DRAFT	MOVIES OF THE MIND: MY EXPERIENCE OF BETSY'S DRAFT
full of Christmas books. I read them over and over again. When I finally read the Polar Express by myself I was so proud. It was a sad day for me when reading became work. I had loved the fulfillment of turning the pages and reading the books for fun, but then reading was a requirement, and I no longer liked it. I began to struggle with reading, and my comprehension. I read very slowly and still did not understand what I read, it was very frustrating.	*of the text, but I can't completely extricate my teacher-self, which is starting to suspect that perhaps Betsy wasn't quite sure what she was writing about when she started—or maybe changed her mind as she wrote. I guess that being a teacher is part of my experience, not something I can extricate. I know that I'm off on a tangent about myself, not paying attention to Betsy's writing, which might mean I'm not fully pulled despite that wicker basket. I need to focus on Betsy's draft.*

Betsy's fourth paragraph:

Sophomore year came to a close, and I would come back from summer a junior. Immediately I knew junior year meant Outback and I did not want to go back, but that was not an option. The fall went by quickly, snow began to fall, the days shortened, darkness loomed, and OB was approaching. I went on numerous trips to EMS to make sure I had everything I was going to need. I had all my friends write me letters, and before I left, I got myself so worked up and anxious that I made myself sick, therefore; I brought lots of medicine. I was determined to bring everything I could need, but of course that was not possible.

My experience of Betsy's fourth paragraph:

OK, we're back to Outback now. That second sentence reminds me of the first, with the drive-by of images, this time about the seasons going by quickly into OB. And again, I'm feeling the ominousness, with darkness looming. It's interesting to have friends write letters. When she mentions that she made herself sick, I'm wondering why she is so anxious. Is there something else going on?

continues

BETSY'S DRAFT	MOVIES OF THE MIND: MY EXPERIENCE OF BETSY'S DRAFT
Betsy's fifth paragraph: For this trip you could not bring any entertainment except for OB letters. The letters were an Outback tradition, and technically you were only supposed to have three letters, but I loved letters and brought all of mine. I knew that was the only way I would make it through. I had thirty-seven letters, from my friends and family, this was an outrageous number, but I treasured my bag of letters, and even before I opened them I felt my connection to home keeping me safe.	**My experience of Betsy's fifth paragraph:** *Aha, we're still on the letters, and I'm getting interested now. The line about thirty-seven letters has me smiling. She's right, that is an outrageous number of letters, and I want to know what they say. I'm feeling like this is the first paragraph that I can really dig into something, and I want to know more.*

With three paragraphs left, I was almost ready to give a suggestion based on the moments I'd been pulled into the essay so far. I could imagine four interesting papers emerging from this draft. One entire essay could be about that red wicker basket full of books. Or about Betsy's experience in Shakespeare class. Or about that English teacher. Or about those letters. These stories could be structured either sequentially or through flashbacks, with explanation and reflection alternating with scenes in different ways—all of which we'd studied during class through examining models and writing exercises. But it was time to let Betsy's intentions streamline and focus my suggestion. So I flipped to the draft note that Betsy had attached to the back of the essay. I'd asked students to describe what felt most "alive" to them, and what felt most "dead." Betsy had written: "The part that feels the most alive to me is talking about my letters and what they meant to me. I don't know if I have shown that alive feeling in my paper, but I tried."

So I asked, "The part of this story that felt the most alive to you was the part about the letters, and that's also the part that felt the most alive to me as a reader. I'm wondering if you wanted to write mostly about those letters?"

That's when Betsy revealed more of her composing story. She had, in fact, wanted to focus on the letters. She didn't think she had enough to say to make a whole essay, however, so she'd added in anything that had to do with literacy. In other words, the story of my reading was a reflection of the story of her writing; I couldn't settle into the essay because she'd shifted from one topic to another for fear of not having enough to say.

I told Betsy that the essay was hers, so although I had a suggestion, she should only consider it if she thought it was going to help her do what she wanted to do. In fact, if it didn't feel right, she should tell me, as that could help me think of a different way to help. "I think I have an idea that will help you do two things you're trying to do at the same time: make this essay all about the letters, and give you a way to have more to say about them. What if you open with the scene of opening the letters—everything you just told me now. That scene was so engaging when you described it to me, and then you can flashback to what led to that moment: the anticipation of going to Holderness, knowing that OB is hanging over your head, and all your experiences and struggles with reading. Because I'll already have read that opening scene about reading those letters, I'll understand those smaller stories as part of this larger (and most important) story about reading for connection and comfort." Betsy seemed excited by the idea, and left to work on revisions. The entire conversation took four minutes. The next class, Betsy handed me her revision. It began like this:

Betsy's Second Draft

Snow was sprinkling the woods, but the sky looked luminous. My tarp was finally set up perfectly, not too close to the path, but not too far away. I was so proud, and I felt ready to conquer my biggest fears, being alone and the dark. I sat cozy in my sleeping bag, under my newly set up

shelter, with my letters dumped all around me. I had thirty-
seven letters, and the ever anticipated moment had finally
arrived. I wanted to rip them all open right then, but I knew
I couldn't. I divided them up so I would have some over each
of the three days. I strategically placed each letter into three
different piles.

I chose one of my best friend Megan's letters to open first.
Megan had written me three letters, one for each night. I
knew that opening hers was the right thing to do because it
would be up beat and keep me positive. As I opened my first
letter, I smiled, colors, magazine clippings, and love came
pouring out of the envelope. It lit me up inside and made me
feel confident in what I was doing. I remember the cut out of
an Abercrombie model she told me to sleep with, giving me a
friend so I was not alone; I think the clipping is probably still
in my sleeping bag.

I had finally made it. I was on Outback, a ten day
camping trip in March where Holderness School's junior
class embarks on a journey in the White Mountains. I
had been petrified of the experience since before I started
Holderness.

My experience of reading this second draft was completely
different. My attention never wandered, and I never wondered what
the wicker basket had to do with camping. Although we'd never
talked about grammar or punctuation, I noticed that Betsy's writing
in this second draft was cleaner. In my experience, that often happens
when the writer finds what she wants to write about. What a waste
of time it would have been to talk about any of these issues in the
first draft! Another reason that writer intention is almost always my
primary concern.

In the next chapter, you'll see movies of the mind weave through
my work with Ben, a young writer. But for now, I'll offer some small
examples of the variety of ways in which movies of the mind shape the
things I say to writers.

Using Movies of the Mind to Work with Writers

- To help the writer clarify intentions/what the piece is about

  o *As I read, I'm most pulled in by the paragraphs about the letters. My mind wanders a bit when I read the explanations of your time at Holderness. I'm trying to figure out if that's because you really wanted to write about the letters—and that's what you should focus on and cut some of the other stories—or if you really want to write about it all, but we need to find a way to make the other descriptions more engaging?*

- To suggest adding more detail

  o *I'm really most interested in those letters—that line about thirty-seven letters got me curious! You're right that it's an outrageous number. When you told me just now about opening the letters in your sleeping bag, I could actually picture that in a way that's not there on the page. If you write a scene—almost like you're making a movie and the camera zooms in so that the audience sees you, surrounded by those letters in your tent on the mountain—that might help me see the moment the way that you experienced it.*

  o *You write here that "it was just an ordinary family dinner." But I don't actually know what an ordinary family dinner is like for you. Is everyone quiet? Talking over each other? Does your mom ask everyone how their day was and everyone rolls their eyes and says, "Fine"? I know what a family dinner is like for me, so all I can do is project that onto this line. Can you give a detail or two that defines ordinary in your family? It could be an entire description, if it's important to setting up the unordinariness that is to come. Or, it could just be a phrase or two to give us a little glimpse of what's ordinary for you.*

- To suggest deletions

  o *On one hand, all these examples of your struggle with reading are really interesting on their own. But I when I read them one after the other, I find myself zoning out by the third example. I think that's because all the examples are illustrating exactly the same point—that you hated reading in school. Maybe the thing to do is to pick the strongest example—or pick more than one if the second one illustrates a different point that you also want to emphasize.*

continues

- To describe how or why something in the text works

  o *I see you've got a flashback structure going here. That works really well for me, because when I read that first little opening scene where you're angry at your friend, it doesn't seem like a significant moment. Frankly, I can't figure out why you're so angry. But as soon as you start describing the backstory—all the moments that led to this opening exchange—I start reading more and more significance into it. So, by the time you get back to that opening scene at the very end, I totally get why you're so angry. The flashback structure really helps you show me how and why such a small, simple moment isn't actually so simple.*

You'll notice that these responses aren't really praise or criticism, indications of the teacher's position of judgment over the student. Instead, these responses position the teacher as the student's ally.

Rather than comparing the writing to a standard, teacher and student negotiate the space between the writer's intention and the reader's experience. The responses might help the writer to make immediate improvements in the draft. But most importantly, such responses are grounded in the reality of the transaction between writer, text, and reader. Therefore, they're capable of nurturing a writer's relationship with audience, and thus, supporting the long-term growth of the writer. Developing voices that are worthy of internalizing, then, involves looking at the writer and the writing through the intention and audience lenses.

7

Writers Are People, Not Pac-Mans

The Stories of One Writer's Growth

I was mostly disinterested in the Atari that my brother got for Christmas in the late 1970s; the excruciatingly slow back-and-forth of *Pong* bored me. But when *Pac-Man* was released in 1982, I was intrigued; fleeing a ghost made sense to me. Still, I was confused by Pac-Man's motivation when it came all to those wafers. One after another, screen after screen, he just kept gobbling them up.

"Why is Pac-Man always so hungry?" I asked my brother while awaiting my turn at the joystick.

His explanation was offered with an exasperated eye roll, "He isn't hungry. You get a point for each one."

In the mainstream vision of "assessment FOR teaching and learning" that I described in Chapter 1, students write for the same reason that Pac-Man munches: to accumulate points as they gobble their way through one grade-level screen of wafer-sized learning targets after another. But writers are people, not Pac-Mans. We don't write to hit learning targets, or to bask in the "whakka" sound of a successfully eaten wafer, or to avoid the weird warble of death by ghost. Instead, we write because we're human, and *writing is a way of seeing and feeling and hearing, a way of asking and knowing, a way of creating and making sense, of expressing and communicating.* If and when we need feedback from another human being, it's to know something of what she experiences when she reads what we write.

To grow as a writer, then, is to grow as a person who uses the written word to see, feel, hear, ask, know, create, make sense, express, and communicate. If assessment misses these fundamental human purposes for writing, it cannot capture a writer's growth, much less support it. Assessment for growth must first recognize that writers are human beings who express and develop their intentions by making decisions about language for an audience of self and others. *This* is the story that assessment must tell writers and everyone involved in the assessment equation. That's what the growth lenses are all about.

At the heart of assessment for growth is the understanding that it's the *person* who grows. I didn't fully understand this until I worked with my own children. A teacher's perspective on growth is framed by the way that relationships are structured within schools. A parent's perspective on growth is another matter. For one thing, it's longitudinal.

This chapter is devoted to the story of my son Ben's growth as a writer. It's also the story of how various reading and writing assessments told *him* stories about how writing and reading work. Sometimes he internalized these stories and told them to himself, and sometimes he resisted and rewrote them. Some stories led to growth in the right direction, and some hindered his development. Whether formative or deformative, these assessments—and the stories they told to Ben—have helped to form Ben's relationships with decision making, his intention, the medium of written language, and an audience of self and others.

As I tell Ben's story, I'll be layering in a discussion of our final growth lens: the medium of written language. This includes everything from genre, organization, word choice, and sentence structure to devices such as flashbacks, metaphor, and alliteration. I've purposely saved this lens for last. For one thing, the medium of written language seems the most familiar consideration in writing assessment, so it's tempting to project traditional writing assessment practices onto it. Any correction a teacher makes on a student's essay, after all, is a correction of the writer's use of the medium.

But that's not what I have in mind. Instead, I want to understand how the writer's *relationship* with the medium forms. And we can't understand this relationship without looking through all of the other growth lenses simultaneously. That's because the writer's intentions meet the audience's experience through the medium of written language. Language is socially constructed, after all. So, it all comes together in Ben's story: to understand Ben's relationship with the medium, we have to understand his relationship with his intentions and an audience of self and others.

Building a Relationship with the Medium: Ben's Story

Ben's relationship with the medium of written language was forged in many early experiences and understandings: in the humor, characterization, and dialogue he encountered in episodes of *The Simpsons* (which he endlessly rewatched and frequently quoted); in the hyperbole, intonation, and pacing of the fabulous yarns spun by Amy, a family friend, every time she visited; in the hours that I typed away on my computer while Ben played nearby. These experiences have become part of Ben's sense of purpose, possibility, and expectation when it comes to language. But I'll focus here on his first contact with the written word. This story of Ben as a writer begins with the story of Ben as a reader.

Kindergarten: Errors

Ben is five years old. It's bedtime, and I'm sitting next to him with a book between us. Usually, it's a manual full of naval submarine specs that I try to read with expression even though I don't know what the numbers or abbreviations mean. I keep pushing my own favorites—*Mona the Brilliant* (Holleyman 1993) or *One Morning in Maine* (McCloskey 1976)—but, night after night, Ben prefers the specs.

Tonight, however, the ritual has changed in one important way. For the first time, Ben is about to read a book to me. The book he's chosen isn't about a submarine, but it's still a perfect fit: the main character's name is Ben, and both the Ben in the book and my Ben have pet birds. When he finishes the story, I'm elated, imagining the paths our conversation might take. Perhaps we'll revel in the similarities between him and the main character or brainstorm what he'll read next. Instead, he closes the book, looks over at me, and asks, "Mom, how many errors did I make?"

Errors? This isn't how I thought this story would end. I've never used the word *error* with Ben. For one thing, I'd never frame a beginning reader's stumbles as anything other than miraculous strides forward. For another thing, I find the word *error* oddly technical. I can't imagine where Ben has heard it, much less internalized and applied it to his reading performance.

First Grade: DIBELS

It's fall, and Ben's principal is on the phone. She explains that Ben has tested below grade level in reading and she wants to put him in a remedial reading class. I ask, "What does it mean to be 'below grade level' during the first week of first grade?" That's when she rattles off the assessments that have been used to determine his placement. As a high school teacher, I don't recognize any of them, but one sounds like something from Lewis Carroll's "Jabberwocky": *dibbles*.

When I google it later that evening, I discover that *dibbles* isn't a word but an acronym: DIBELS, for Dynamic Indicators of Basic Early Literacy Skills. And it isn't a single test, but a "battery of probes." As I learn about it, Ben's strange question last year comes into focus. For the DIBELS fluency probe, each child is handed a paper with a series of nonsense syllables (*sim, lut, vag,* and so on). Armed with a stopwatch and clipboard, the examiner commands the child to read the nonsense as quickly as possible. Every time the child mispronounces a sound, the examiner makes a slash through the corresponding syllable on his copy of the probe ("and with his vorpal sword goes snicker-snack!"). When one minute is up, these slashes are added up and divided by the total number possible to calculate the "error rate" (Good and Kaminski 2002, 24–25).

There it is: *error*. The more I dig into the various assessments used in my son's classroom, the more the word shows up. Elementary teachers in the district tell me that they are required to administer most of these assessments once a month from kindergarten through fifth grade, and one teacher has counted up the time required: a third of the school year. Some reading assessments require the children to chart and track their own errors. Finally, Ben's question makes perfect sense. At school, his stumbles have regularly been identified as errors and counted against him.

These assessments—the stopwatch, the slash through his errors, the nonsense, for god's sake!—have told Ben a powerful story about what good readers do and why they do it. *Good readers read fast. Good readers don't make any mistakes. Readers read to score better on tests of isolated subskills. And good readers don't bother with meaning.* It doesn't much matter whether his teachers personally believe this story. It's the story the assessments tell, and it's the story Ben hears. Even at home, with an interesting book in front of him and an interested listener who has never scored anything he has ever done, this story proves stubborn and strong. Ben has learned to tell it to himself, and it underlies the question he asks me: "Mom, how many errors did I make?"

Second Grade: Six-Minute Solution and AR

As I wait for Ben's second-grade parent-teacher conference, I peruse the student work lining the hallways, including responses to this prompt: *My favorite subject is . . .* Writing isn't mentioned anywhere, but I make a beeline to the single "I Love Reading" gracing the wall. However, its second-grade author doesn't describe or even mention a single book. Instead, he writes about how much he liked watching the scores rise on his Six-Minute Solution chart, how upset he had been when he could only read 53 words per minute, and how excited he felt when he reached 200.

I don't know anything about Six-Minute Solution, so I ask Ben's teacher about it when it's my turn for the conference. She opens Ben's folder, pulls out his Six-Minute Solution chart, and explains. Minute one: the teacher announces it is time for fluency practice. Kids retrieve their fluency folders, find their partners, pull out a leveled passage, and record the date on their charts. Minute two: the teacher sets a timer and says, "Go!" Kids read from the leveled passage as fast as they can while their partners record their errors. Minute three: The teacher says, "Stop!" Midpassage or midsentence, readers stop reading and mark their spot in the passage. Partners calculate the student's reading rate (number of words attempted minus errors), perform the "error correction procedure," and chart the student's score. Partners swap roles, and repeat the procedure. The kids have so much fun with it, the teacher gushes; it's like a race.

The comment is custom-made for a Deweyan analysis. The students may very well experience the assessment as "immediately enjoyable" (Dewey 1938, 13). However, this is not the same as saying that it leads the students to be eager and receptive to future reading—if, by *reading*, we mean *sensemaking*. This might explain why the author of "I Love Reading" didn't make the leap from celebrating his scores to describing the actual books he'd read. It's a miseducative experience, leading to growth in the wrong direction.

This also helps to explain what happens next in the conference, when I ask what kind of books Ben enjoys reading at school. That's when his teacher pulls out a list of his Accelerated Reader (AR) comprehension scores. Next to each score (determined by a ten-question multiple-choice quiz) is the book Ben chose to read: each is from the Arthur the Aardvark series. I'm surprised, because I've tried unsuccessfully to read Arthur books to Ben at home. Maybe his tastes have changed.

When I return home after the conference, I ask Ben if he likes Arthur books now. His answer is an emphatic *no*. Instead, he explains, Arthur books are the best value in the AR system. They have a high point value but you can basically look at the pictures, pass the tests, and thereby accumulate the necessary number of points per quarter.

Every experience lives on in future experiences, and every story lives on in future stories. The story Ben heard loud and clear in kindergarten and first grade is being repeated in second grade, and is bearing its misdirected fruit. *Good readers read fast. Good readers don't make any mistakes. Readers read to score better on tests of isolated subskills. And good readers don't bother with meaning.* This year, thanks to AR, there's a new twist: Ben has figured out how to do all of this without reading much at all. He's reading like a Pac-Man, gobbling up points because, well, that's what the game is.

Fourth Grade: Drawn in by Dahl

It isn't until fourth grade at a new school that Ben begins to revise this troubling story about reading. I attribute this revision to his fourth-grade teacher. A thirty-year veteran of education, she runs a class newspaper and has a sprawling classroom library. Just as importantly, she refuses to give the reading assessments that the school has mandated as part of its push for data-driven education. (I learn about this when the teacher unexpectedly retires halfway through the year, and the principal mentions that it's a *good* thing she has retired since she refused to comply. I point out how much Ben learned from her, suggesting that her refusal to give the assessments may have allowed for this learning, but the point is lost on the principal.)

In the months before her retirement, however, this teacher lets the kids read what they want. Recognizing Ben's sense of humor (he still regularly quotes extensive passages of dialogue from *The Simpsons*), she introduces him to Roald Dahl. Without a point system to game, Ben is finally free to be reeled into reading by Dahl's weird wit. Once it starts, it happens fast, and he spends many late nights reading *The Twits*, followed by Lemony Snicket's A Series of Unfortunate Events, and, eventually, Susan Collins' The Hunger Games series. He's a bit young for the violent dystopia, but his older brother has been raving about the series, and I worry that to slow him down now would be to turn the books into contraband. He tells me that he cried when Prim dies in *Mockingjay*, and he didn't realize before that books could make you cry. In fact, he's started rereading the book already.

No longer focused on his errors or an elaborate point system that draws his attention away from meaning, Ben is free to form empathetic relationships with authors and their characters—and with others, like his brother, who have formed similar relationships. Without the interference of a bevy of deformative reading assessments, Ben is hearing (and starting to tell himself) a different story about reading. *Readers read to laugh and to cry. Readers read because authors and characters speak to them. Readers are carried through "errors" by meaning. Readers reread and engage differently each time. Readers read to connect with other readers.* This story was available to him all the time; I was certainly trying to tell it to him. But it was drowned out by a school-sponsored story that gained its power not from the collective experience of readers, but from the power invested in institutional assessment.

Fifth Grade: Spelling Tests and a Survival Story

On the first day of fifth grade at yet another school, Ben chooses the seat closest to the bookcase "to be closer to all the books." He's starting to see himself as a reader, and I'm wondering when evidence of Ben's newfound connection with reading will show up in his writing: a dash of Dahl's gobblefunk, or the steampunk of a Snicket setting, or the inner conflict of a Collins character. When Ben's older brother Isaiah was in first grade, I saw this reading-writing connection emerge very clearly.

I first noticed it after Isaiah and I finished reading the American Chillers series. In each book, a young protagonist defends his or her hometown from villainous machines, toys, or beasts that come to life to wreak havoc. They also alliterate with whatever state the story takes place: *Terrible Tractors of Texas, Dangerous Dolls of Delaware, The Michigan Mega-Monsters,* and so on. When Isaiah learned that he was supposed to write a Young Authors book for school, he titled it, "Isaiah and the Zero Blaster." He made himself the protagonist, wielding a toy he'd gotten for Christmas that blasts purple smoke rings (the aptly named "zero blaster") to battle a monster that tried to take over his hometown. But Isaiah adopted more than the plotline of American Chillers. He also borrowed a suspense-building technique employed liberally in the series: a two-sentence turn in which everything *seems* normal . . . until . . . it's not. ("Every summer we have a blast. [line break] Except for this summer.")

However, there's not much evidence of Ben's reading to be seen in his writing yet. This is mostly because he hasn't done much writing at school or at home. With a dearth of actual composing experience, he equates writing with two subjects that feature more regularly in the curriculum: spelling and handwriting. With lots of time and help, Ben can remember how to spell some new words on the weekly lists, but rarely enough to pass the tests. In addition, his large unruly handwriting spills over the lines. I've seen versions of the same handwriting in many of my high school students—mostly males—and it's almost always punished in school; it paints the writer as childish, no matter how sophisticated the content. I hoped that access to a computer would help, but Ben struggles with fine motor skills on the keyboard, too. No matter how many times I tell him that spelling and handwriting aren't the same as writing, he believes they are. He tells himself (and anyone who asks) that he is bad at all three.

Now that Ben has so many beloved books to draw on, I'm just waiting for an interesting writing project to come home. I love working with resistant writers in my own classroom, and although I know from painful experience that helping your own kids with their homework is different than teaching students in your own classroom, I'm willing to try. Lucky for both of us, I don't have to wait long. Ben's fifth-grade teacher is a longtime member of the National Writing Project, and within a month he's sent home an extended project that I wish I'd thought of for my own classroom. By this time, however, Ben's perception of himself as a writer is so negative that I don't even hear about the project until he's sitting at the dining room table in tears, convinced that he can't do it.

The details of the assignment emerge slowly, but I finally get the story. For the last several weeks, students have read different survival stories in small groups, and Ben's group has read *Julie of the Wolves* by Jean Craighead George (1972). They've talked about the research the authors would have done to create the settings, characters, and action in the books. I open to the first page of *Julie of the Wolves* and am struck by the number of facts embedded in these few opening sentences:

> *Miyax pushed back the hood of her sealskin parka and looked at the Arctic sun. It was a yellow disc in a lime-green sky, the colors of six o'clock in the evening and the time when the wolves awoke. Quietly she put down her cooking pot and crept to the top of a dome-shaped frost heave, one of the*

many earth buckles that rise and fall in the crackling cold of the Arctic winter. (1972, 5)

They've finished reading the book, and now they're supposed to be writing their own survival stories. They've already done research on an island, which will become the setting for their story. Ben has picked an island off the coast of the Philippines, and shows me the notes he's taken on his research:

average temperature is 90 degrees.

A sandy beach encircles the island, with marshy forests in the middle.

The island has mangrove trees, banana trees, and alligators.

A photograph of a mangrove tree printed from the Internet is taped to his notes.

When I finally get a sense of the assignment, I tell Ben that it sounds like a cool project and that it also looks like he's gotten a lot done already. But my cheeriness is lost on him. He's frustrated and says he can't write. When I ask why, he tells me that he's a terrible speller. I say, "We can fix spelling later. Let's just focus on your story," and I ask him about his plan so far. He tells me that he wants his character to be stranded in a plane crash, like Brian in Gary Paulsen's *Hatchet* (1987), but he doesn't know how to begin.

I ask Ben to close his eyes and imagine that he's just crashed on the island himself. He obliges, and I ask what he sees. Is he conscious? He says no; he tells me he would have blacked out on impact. I ask him to imagine the moment of waking up. What would he see first? As he answers, I transcribe exactly what he says: "My head hurt. My body ached. I slowly opened my eyes. Everything was blurry. I blinked. My vision slowly came back."

I remind Ben that he's the only one who can see what happened to his character. If he wants his audience to see it, too, he has to describe it on paper just like he described it to me. I hand him the paper with the six sentences I've just transcribed, and ask him to read it. Does he like it? He says, "It's OK." I tell him that it makes me want to know more as a reader because those few sentences have a big mystery embedded in them. What just happened to make his vision blurry? What does he see once his vision comes back? I want to keep reading to figure out what the mystery is. I tell him to keep writing.

Ben works steadily (no more tears!) for the next half hour or so, a record for him. I stop him before he's run out of steam. I'm tempted to let him keep going—why wake a sleeping child or interrupt a writing child?—but I vaguely remember advice that Donald Murray is reported to have given: always stop in the middle of a sentence, so that when you come back to your writing the next day, you start with momentum. Plus, it's getting late. When Ben hands me what he's been working on, he seems pleased.

A draft is due tomorrow morning, so I type it for him, careful to transcribe every misspelling and mispunctuation. I'm walking a very fine scaffolding line here, taking over some of the mechanical aspects of the task that add to his frustration so he can experience the work of getting his meaning into words. Still, I know he needs help paying attention to those mundane details. My compromise, then, is to type it for him, but ask him to read it line by line and correct anything that doesn't look right to him. My hypothesis is that he knows many of the conventions, but doesn't bother to pay attention.

This work—rereading and editing—happens excruciatingly slowly. I have to stop Ben and tell him to reread a sentence many times before he notices what needs to change, and sometimes I show him how to do something, such as indenting dialogue to show the shifts in speaker. My plan to end the evening with some momentum is blown, and I'm worried about whether the work is becoming too disagreeable to be educative, but he is hanging in there with me. By the time we break for bed, he's got this draft to hand in tomorrow:

Ben's Survival Story

My head hurt. My body ached. I slowly opened my eyes. Everything was blurry. I blinked. My vision slowly came back. I noticed that I was on a sandy beach. I was in an ejection seat. Then I remembered that I was in a plane crash with another pilot.

I tried to get up but I couldn't. I looked at my leg then I noticed that my leg had a big bump. I thought, "Oh god!" At that moment I saw the other pilot. I yelled, "Help!" He looked up and ran over to me.

He said, "Are you ok?"

"I think I hurt my leg." Then he noticed the bump on my leg. He dragged me over to a mangrove tree and got a first aid kit. He got some morphine from the kit and gave it to me.

I sighed in relief. Then he read a piece of paper saying how to fix a dislocated hip. He said, "Let's see if this works." He pushed my hip in. I heard a pop then he said, "Try and stand up." I got up and almost fell over again.

I said, "What's your name?"

"Jack." he replied.

"I'm Gary. What do we have for supplies?"

Jack replied, "Matches, 5 MRE's, flare gun, 2 canteens of water and bandages, that's it."

"Ok we should make a shelter. I'll build it. You bring me some pieces to build with." I chose a spot under a large mangrove. Jack brought a bunch of driftwood and big leaves. I started to make a TP. It took about an hour to build.

Once we were done I was drenched in sweat. It had to have been a full 90 degrees the whole time. I drank some water from the canteen. I went in side the TP and put some banana leaves on the ground where we would sleep.

The next four days were torture. We only had one more MRE and a quarter of a canteen of water. The next day we went into the swamp a couple hundred feet into the swamp and saw water. We left marks on mangrove trees with a knife to mark the way back.

Despite the tears at the beginning, Ben's intention is clearly engaged now. And I'm pleased to see how naturally he's incorporated his research (the sandy beach, temperature, banana and mangrove trees) into his setting. Moreover, I can clearly see little bits of his reading show up in his writing. He's compressed time ("The next four days were torture"), a technique that authors use all the time in the action-driven stories that Ben has spent the past few years reading. In Ben's story, the time compression works to transition us from the first few hours on the island—where every detail of the setting is new and worth telling—deeper into the story where action matters more. Then, there's that morphine! How does a fifth grader know about morphine? Should I be worried? But I remember that "Morphlings" are featured in The Hunger Games—addicts who have turned to drugs to make it through the games. In just these few paragraphs, Ben's newly forged relationship with reading is paying off in his writing.

When Ben gets home from school the next day, he tells me that he and his friend talked about his story during recess and he wrote more after lunch. He's giggling—something about an alligator—so I ask to read. He hands me the new material that he and his friend brainstormed and that he wrote during class:

> I was limping still from the plane crash when we got to the water. I put my finger in the water. I took it out. I tasted it. It was fresh water! I jumped in. Jack said, "Wait, don't move."
> "Why?"
> "Because there is a GATOR behind you." Jack took out the flare gun. The gator had its mouth open waiting for its prey. Earlier we made the shots for the flare gun in to a sharp point. He aimed at the gators mouth and shot. The flare ripped the epiglottis and went into the lungs and exploded! Jack took his knife and cut its head open to make sure that it was dead.
> That evening he skinned it and cut it into chunks..Jack was roasting some meat on a fire. . . .
> That night we ate meat and our last m.r.e. We still had enough meat and water for about 3 weeks at most. The next five days where a repeat of all the other ones, eat, sleep, eat, sleep.

I ask Ben how he know about an epiglottis or an MRE. He says something about the Discovery Channel, but he's running off to grab his soccer ball. I read it again, and after I cringe at the poor alligator's fate, I notice Ben's second use of that time-compressing technique, with a dose of repetition: "The next five days where a repeat of all the other ones, eat, sleep, eat, sleep." It captures the monotony of the experience through repetition, without itself being monotonous.

I don't hear anything more about the story until the next week, when I ask about it. Ben shows me the ending he's written:

> It's been nine days since the plane crash. We stayed up late to watch the stars. I looked at the north star. Suddenly I had an idea. We could build a raft to get back to civilization. I figured we could get it done by morning.
>
> It was a long morning. Around 8:00 we were done. We used the alligator skin as a rope to tie some drift wood as the base. And some styrofoam from the wreck. Then we put the rest of the alligator skin for a flap for shade on the raft. And we tied a long stick with a long fat board we found on the beach for a paddle.
>
> For the first time the boat went in the water. It sank a little. We added some styrofoam to make it so it could withstand our weight. It held together fine. With in an hour the island was gone.
>
> We still had a flare gun, meat and lots of water. With in two days there was a land mass in the distance. It was huge! When we were about half a mile away I saw the rigid coast line. I told Jack that we had to jump to get on the island. A big wave came. It was at least 15 feet tall. I said, "Brace your self!" I took the first aid kit with all our supplies. We leapt and ended up with our boat almost hitting us from the wave. We were on a big green field.
>
> I saw smoke in the distance. We ran to a little cottage. We knocked and someone answered and said, "Are you ok?"
>
> I said, "Call the police station!" The man called and said that they would be here soon. They came in about 15 minutes. I said, "Thank you." and left. The police took us to the hospital. The doctors fixed us up. In a couple of months everyone was fine. We were out of the hospital and back on our feet. Jack and I are still in touch. We get together from time to time and I will never forget this ever again.

In addition to the inventive use of alligator skin, I'm struck by another technique that Ben has picked up from his reading. When I taught this technique to my eleventh graders, I called it "mindsliding." In mindsliding, a character observes an everyday object. These observations morph (or slide) into memories that reveal the character's backstory, or associations that illuminate her personality or state of mind, or actions that propel the story forward. One of my students had used the technique to show how grief sneaks up on you in the most mundane ways. His story began in the middle of one of his tennis matches. As the fuzzy tennis ball came toward him over the net, time slowed down, and he was reminded of his dying grandfather's mostly bald, fuzzy head. The tennis match forgotten, he was back in the hospital with his grandfather. It sounds like a strange connection, but it was extraordinarily effective, illustrating how grief transforms and interrupts reality. Without any direct instruction, Ben is using this technique: "We stayed up late to watch the stars. I looked at the north star. Suddenly, I had an idea."

After I read, Ben tells me about his draft conference with his teacher, who made several suggestions. Some of the suggestions he'll take, such as clarifying the source of the Styrofoam used in the rescue raft. But then Ben scrunches up his nose and reports that he's supposed to cut the alligator scene because it is unrealistic. I ask him what he's going to do. He tells me how he asked his friend to read it after the teacher's suggestion. After discussing the dilemma, they decided together to keep the scene. It's his favorite thing that he's ever written.

His teacher is right: the scene is unrealistic. But Ben's refusal to take the suggestion strikes me as a healthy sign. He's not writing like Pac-Man, collecting points to win the game. Instead, he's making decisions based on his intentions, informed by his reading, his television watching, his own sense of humor and drama, and consultations with multiple audiences. Even though his decision might cost him with the one audience authorized to award or withhold points, he's writing more for himself and his friend than for his teacher or me. That may not bode well for his grade, but it bodes well for his development as a writer.

Seventh Grade: "I walked and walked until my legs could walk no more."

Ben is now in seventh grade, and he is sitting on the couch with his computer. He hasn't brought much writing home to work on since fifth grade. At the end of sixth grade, he showed me the journal he kept in class, a wild collection of hand-drawn comics and stream-of-consciousness rantings intended only for him. But this year, his social studies class has been studying the Trail of Tears, and they've read numerous firsthand accounts from children's diaries and letters. Now, they're supposed to write an historical fiction piece that includes details from their learning.

Ben says he doesn't know how to begin, but there are no tears this time. Remembering the strategy that worked to kick off his survival story, I say, "Just imagine yourself *there* and start writing about what you see and think and feel." He begins without hesitation and writes for about twenty minutes, then hands his computer to me. The first several sentences, centered in the middle of the screen, read:

> *Its hard to beleve that its been 1 year sence we got to*
> *oklahoma I can remember the day like I can see through*
> *the air. The day started off peaceful and clear. The crisp air*
> *that blew off the mountians filling my mouth as i breathed,*
> *I herd some horses off in the distance I figured It was my*
> *father riding back from the hunt .*

Two parts of me react simultaneously. The first part of me has her breath taken away. Ben opens with a flashback, a technique definitely inspired by his reading: he's in Oklahoma, thinking back to how he got there. And he's got that unique sensory detail right at the beginning that creates an almost mystical tone: "I can remember the day like I can see through the air." Then, he introduces the tragedy to come indirectly, through another sensory detail that transports the reader into another time period: "I herd some horses off in the distance I figured It was my father riding back from the hunt." I feel like I've entered the mind of a narrator who sees and feels the world in a unique way, and I'm happy to stay in that world and eager to find out what he experiences next.

But the second part of me is worried. Not everyone is as willing as I am to read through Ben's spelling, punctuation, capitalization, and even spacing—nor should they be. Ben is in seventh grade. In fact, Ben's social studies teacher this year is also his English language arts teacher, and she recently requested that Ben be tested for special education services based on writing samples she collected from his tests. She shared these samples at a meeting and they're very short constructed responses, written in his large messy handwriting and strewn with the same kind of errors that mark the first sentences of this story. There are some fascinating turns of phrase, but she brushes them off when I point them out. Her concern is about conventions and length.

I don't disagree with her; Ben needs to practice editing strategies. All I can think to do is to read each sentence out loud and ask him what looks wrong, like we did several years ago. With enough practice, he should be able to do this himself. Still, I know how laborious this process is—for both of us. It can easily overshadow the creative aspects of composing, which Ben has just started to experience. Can both parts of me find a way forward without stumbling over one another?

It's time to bring in an audience of others. This idea isn't without risk: I don't want to shame Ben into fixing his errors. But I do want to introduce a rhetorical situation that isn't fraught with three possible complications of writing for the teacher: judgment; the power imbalance of the teacher-student relationship; or disinterest through familiarity. I'm currently teaching two fourth- through eighth-grade literacy methods courses at the university. The preservice teachers in my classes have been exploring two related pedagogical issues—honoring a student's intention and reading for potential—and we're always in need of actual student writing. So, I'm in a position to broker a mutually beneficial exchange. I ask Ben if I can share his writing with my students. They could write him letters about his story, and he could give them feedback on the kind of responses that are helpful to him.

Ben agrees. In the next few days, he finishes a draft to share with my students. As we read and reread each line, we ask whether the college students will understand. He writes this draft, which I share with my students

The Trail of Tears

*It's hard to believe that it's been 1 year since we got
to Oklahoma. I can remember the day as clear as the
mountain streams. The day started off peaceful and clear.
The crisp air that blew off the mountains filled my mouth
as I breathed.*

*I heard some horses off in the distance. I figured it was my
father riding back from the hunt. I ran out to the pasture to
greet him but instead of my father, there were two white men
riding toward me, their guns raised. I sprinted to the house,
screaming and yelling, but it was too late. They had already
grabbed my hair and dragged me to the horse pen, along
with many people in my tribe.*

*As the white men cleared out our homes taking all our
jewelry and valuables my father was thrown over the fence
and hit his head on a rock. He was limp when I got to him.
His head had blood trickling down, creating a small pool on
the ground. I said his name lightly, then louder and louder
until I was screaming. My friend came over and dragged me
from my father. Tears streamed down my face.*

*We stayed in the pen which felt like weeks. Then a white
man came and started yelling something in a different
language and opened the gate. As we filed into lines my
mother hugged me tight. That was the start of a thousand
mile treck through the worst winter in a long time.*

*It felt like months but had only been a week with my
mother still clinging to me. Hundreds of my people have died
and many more to come. The nights were freezing, some
without blankets. We would huddle together in tight groups
to keep warm. One fateful morning I woke. My mother was
cold she did not produce the same heat that she had to keep
me warm during the past month.*

*I was in shock. I was mad and sad at the same time. I
didn't know what was going on. I wanted to die from the
sadness of losing both my parents. As my friend and my*

relatives buried my mother in a shallow grave I reviewed
what my parents and I had gone through.

    I walked and walked and walked until my legs could walk
no more. As I dropped to the ground my friend came to my
aid. I blacked out and I was no more

    When I woke we weren't moving, I noticed that I was
warm and on a soft bed with sheets. I tried to get up but my
legs were stiff. My uncle came into the room his face lit up
with joy and relief as he saw me look at him. He came and
gave me the hug that made my eyes pop out of my sockets.

    He explained that I blacked out and slept for two weeks
and we were in Oklahoma. I stumbled to the flap of the tent
and looked out. My eyes hurt as they adjusted to the light. I
saw lots of tents and cabins being built on the clearing. I was
happy but sad. I was happy to be there but sad to have left
the place that I knew so well.

    The next week in class, I share the story of Ben's composing
process. We read his drafts out loud, and then my students narrate
"movies of the mind" to each other. Then they craft letters to Ben,
which I take home and read to him. He identifies this letter from Alex
as helpful:

> Ben,
>
> You are crazy to think you are a bad writer because
> you are not a good speller! . . . I could tell you were
> very invested in this writing . . . and it sounded like
> you knew what you were talking about from the
> book you read and any extra research you did . . . I
> can actually feel myself in these scenes . . . when you
> describe your mother clinging to you and the cold
> nights, some without blankets, I can feel the tragedy
> and see the horrific scene. You really helped me see
> and feel this story through your descriptions . . .
>
> Alex

When I ask why he finds this letter helpful, Ben says, "Because she called me crazy." Then he laughs and says, "No, it's because maybe I can write." In the end, the low grade that Ben receives on his paper and the circled feedback on the rubric matter less to him than the forty letters he has from college students. The teacher has her reasons for the grade, and that's fine, but what matters to me is that Ben's relationship with the medium, with his intentions, and with his audience is becoming stronger. In other words, he's growing as a writer.

A Coda: The Dignity of Shorts

Ben loves his eighth-grade English teacher this year, who laughs at his jokes and does "interesting stuff" in class. After reading David Sedaris essays for the past month (Ben's choice), the assignment is to write something inspired by his reading. When Ben tells me the due date, I invite him on a Saturday to the coffeehouse, where I've been finishing my dissertation. We set up with drinks (coffee for me, Jones Soda for Ben) and our laptops.

This time when I ask what he wants to write, Ben's already got a first sentence planned. He recites it for me, and I smile; it's got Sedaris written all over it. We both get to work. Several pastries and hours later, he's done. There are very few errors, and while he'll make a few revisions in the days to come, it's almost in final draft shape:

Dignity

Shorts are a symbol of your dignity and I was about to lose mine. The coral beaches scraped my bare feet and caused me to hunch over in pain like a middle aged person walking on black ice. The weather was warm and savory. The pain of the coral was relieved by the soft hot sand. My dad, brother and I found a suitable place to set ourselves and then we started to get ready to swim in the surf. Dad warned me of the under toe and told me to only swim sideways to it. My feet were burning so I ran to the water and jumped in.

This was my first time in Mexico and the warmth had overwhelmed me once I got off the plane. I remember driving to the mud made small apartments that many tourists had visited before me. My family was greeted by our friends and the couple that lived there with their son Diego. Diego and my brother became quite fond of each other and they bonded quickly over music. Diego would guide us to my lifeline . . . the pool. I ended up spending over seventy percent of my time in that pool, only coming out to eat and sleep and occasionally take a leak or poop. My skin started to become like my grandmother's so I decided to try something new.

Dad, my brother, and I walked to the beach to go swimming. The palms that lined the beach were full of coconuts and lizards. One of the lizards caught my eye so I ran to it. The lizard was massive. Half the size of me, it blended into the tree. I was deeply mesmerized so I did what every child would do. I picked up a rock and I threw it at the lizard. It looked at me as the small rock bounced off of its tail. Then it scurried off of the palm onto the sand.

What captivated me about this strange creature was once it touched the sand it changed into the color to blend in. My jaw dropped in amazement. How could this creature change color? So as any eight year old boy would do I imagined my self changing color. I could be lizard man and I could be a super hero and climb all over people and save them from the bad guys. Then my train of thought was shattered by the realization that my dad and brother were off in the distance. So I ran to catch up.

That's when I found myself jumping into the water to escape the burning sand. The warm water was delightful. I had not developed the fear of sea creatures like jellyfish and sea urchin so I swam undeterred by the dangers and enjoyed myself. I attacked the waves like I was fighting for my life. They were the bad guys in my awesome lizard fantasy. The surfers skimmed the water like water flies. Some of the waves were massive to an eight year old and even to an adult they were still big. The waves would roll in and crash against the far beach and the occasional break would come to where we were and sweep me off my feet towards the beach.

My father and I then waded farther out. Then the wave that I lost my dignity to came. The massive wave had grown enough to even intimidate my father so he started dragging me to shore. The currents that the wave produced were tremendous to an eight year old and I struggled to clutch to my father's hands. In one brief moment I realized that there was no hope in the world as my shorts were sucked off my pelvis. I was sure that they would be sucked out to sea and I would never see them again. My eyes opened and I saw my nobility clutching to my left foot as if they were toying with me.

I looked at my dad like I was about to cry then I looked at the thousands of locals that were intently staring at the "typical" American family like there was no hope in our country. Somehow the shorts remained clutching to my toes as the water rushed in. I immediately slipped them back on and tightened the ties and continued fighting the waves as if nothing had happened. My brother was boisterously laughing his head off and my dad was chuckling along with the other thousands of people that lined the beach. Once my skin again looked like my grandmother's so I decided to head back home in search of another awesome experience.

I'm laughing all the way through Ben's story. Shortly, I might offer a movie of the mind, especially when it comes to the suspense of the first sentence or the fantasy of the superhero lizard scene. But the assessment I am most interested in making in this moment has little to do with Ben's use of detail, humor, or "mindsliding." Instead, it's about Ben's growth as a writer. Ben's relationships with decision making, his intentions, an audience of self and others, and the medium of written language are on solid ground. I have no numbers to offer, and I won't compare him to any of his peers. Nonetheless, I am confident in my assessment: Ben is growing in the right direction. Isn't that the entire point?

Practicing Assessment in the Gaps

No institution or ideology has complete control over human thought and activity, so we don't need to wait for the entire system to change to work toward assessment that supports growth in the right direction. There are gaps in the system—small, hidden spaces in which to evade, ignore, resist, and reframe assessment mandates. Here are some insights I've gleaned from two decades of practicing assessment in the gaps.

Reduce the frequency and importance of grades.

There are many ways to work toward deemphasizing grades. None are perfect, and some methods work better than others in different settings. Possibilities include the following:

- Don't grade first drafts. Allow feedback and revisions to be free of the pressure of grades until both teacher and student are ready for it to be graded.

- Give all-or-nothing participation points for participation in the writing process, including timely completion of drafts and consideration of feedback. (For a description of Linda Christensen's [2004–2005] version of this grading scheme, see "Moving Beyond Judgment.")

- Don't grade any drafts: Negotiate a final course grade based on a grading contract. For more, see "A Unilateral Contract to Improve Learning and Teaching" (Elbow 2008).

Some parents think they want rubrics because they fear you're going to use grades to punish or surprise. If you don't, they'll often embrace an ungraded (or less-graded) classroom.

There's power in organizing.

In 2009, the Seattle Public Schools adopted the Measures of Academic Progress (MAP) test, administered three times a year in addition to state-mandated tests. When high school teacher Mallory Clarke explained to her colleagues why she refused to give the MAP test, they understood and brought their concerns to the administration. Their efforts culminated in a nationally publicized boycott that eventually involved seven schools and garnered the support of many parents in the district. The MAP test was eventually pulled from the high school. There's much to learn from these teachers about the power of collective action, and you can read their account in *More Than a Score: The New Uprising Against High-Stakes Testing* (Hagopian 2014).

Vigilance is important: the gaps have sneaky ways of shrinking.

Sometimes, when a school considers a new program, such as the Dufour Model of Professional Learning Communities, hidden assessment mandates are embedded in them that might affect your classroom assessment practices. It's better to study and understand these early, while you have a chance of affecting their adoption. See Chris Gallagher and Eric Turley's (2012) account of my own experience with this in *Our Better Judgment: Teacher Leadership in Assessment*.

If there's no way to get it right (and there isn't!), I'll choose the ways in which I get it wrong.

I know—from experience and research—that grades undermine the kind of learning and writing that I want to cultivate in my classroom. Do my attempts to deemphasize grades lead to grade inflation? I sometimes worry about this, but then I remember that the destructive effects of grades worry me more. Because I'm confident that deemphasizing grades facilitates deeper learning for more students, I'll accept the so-called problem of grade inflation.

8

How the Growth Lenses Can Help Us Teach

I remember the first time I heard the phrase "assessment that informs instruction." It was 2005. I was a seventh-year teacher, and I'd joined a small group of English teachers assembled by the regional Intermediate School District (ISD), which consisted of five school districts in the county. Our mission? To standardize the ninth-grade English curriculum and assessments across the five districts. It wasn't a mission I was particularly enthused about. Still, I'd volunteered for it. For one thing, the ISD always provided great snacks. For another thing, I'd actually joined the group with the intention of stopping it.

Our task for the afternoon was to choose a common rubric. To introduce this task, the ISD leader gave a minilecture on assessment. She began by asking if anyone knew the difference between summative and formative assessment. No one did. In her explanation, she admitted that she had a hard time keeping the two separate, so she offered us the trick she used herself: a **sum**mative assessment often contains a **sum** (such as a grade), and **form**ative assessments are used to in**form** instruction.

Assessments that inform instruction. Apparently, the common rubric would inform our instruction. After we all administered the same writing prompt, we'd gather together and score the writing with the same rubric, and that process would tell us what we needed to teach next. If we noticed, for instance, that students in our class struggled with transition words, we'd then know to do a minilesson on transition words.

As much as I objected to the conclusion that we needed a common assessment to inform instruction (as if I weren't already responsive to my students' needs), I was drawn to the phrase. *Assessment that informs instruction.* It's catchy. And it sounds cool. *Informs* and *instruction* roll into the shared *n*'s, *r*'s and *s*'s. So cool, in fact, that I considered using it now to capture what I want to talk about next: using the growth lenses to help us teach. Besides being catchy, the phrase is firmly entrenched in the mainstream discourse. Using it to frame my own ideas might serve to make them more easily acceptable. I need all the help I can get.

However, the phrase makes a telling semantic omission that I simply can't ignore. Like the passively constructed sentence, it obfuscates. *Assessment that informs instruction.* Notice that there is no human actor in this phrase, no teacher who assesses or instructs. Instead, *assessment* is the actor that informs. And teachers aren't even the object of the sentence; assessment doesn't inform *teachers*, it informs *instruction*. In this formulation, instruction is externalized, existing outside any particular exchange between teacher and student. If we do imagine an implied teacher hovering around the margins of this phrase, she is rendered passive, controlled by the assessment and disconnected from her instruction.

The erasure and domination of the teacher in this phrase is not merely semantic or metaphoric. Educational policy ignores teachers' voices in the national educational discourse, treating them as problems to be solved, variables to be controlled, and villains to be held accountable through standards and testing. And, in its search for a model of instruction to "scale up," the reform movement separates teachers from the contextual reality of their own particular classrooms, making instruction a commodity rather than a unique exchange between teachers, students, communities, methods, and materials. It is just such a deskilled teacher to whom Culham's feedback is packaged and sold.

So, it's taken over a decade, but I'm now officially over the phrase, *assessment that informs teaching*. But I still want to talk about how the growth lenses can affect what teachers do with and for students. In the absence of an equivalently catchy phrase, I'll invoke our biologically inspired metaphor to frame this discussion: a writer's DNA.

Within this metaphor, we all have what it takes to learn to compose, even before we learn to write, but we need supportive environments in which our expressive, creative, and social decision-making core can develop. If this is true, remediation or intervention isn't the logical response to assessment with the growth lenses. That's because these lenses aren't designed to diagnose deficiencies in individual writers. We wouldn't look at a pale, scrawny seedling and decide that we need to deliver a minilesson on photosynthesis, admonish it to work harder, and do a few grit exercises. Instead, we'd add nutrients to the soil, or clear out whatever blocked its light, or water it more (or less). The problem probably isn't the seed, in other words; the problem is that the environment isn't supporting the seed's growth.

The same is true for writers. The point of looking through the growth lenses isn't to decide that the student hasn't grown, deliver minilessons on the deficiencies, admonish the writer to work harder, and dangle a grade over her head to motivate more effort. The point is to understand the relationships and experiences that constitute a writer's decision-making core. If we suspect that these relationships don't support growth in the right direction, we can design experiences and environments that nurture them. It's indirect work that takes time. But growth in the right direction unfolds over time, anyway.

Supporting Students to Develop Healthy Decision-Making Relationships

There is no one right learning environment for each student, but here are some ideas that I've found to support students in developing healthy decision-making relationships with their intentions, their audiences, and the medium of language:

- Model the decisions you make as a writer through write-alouds: coming to and clarifying intention; using and silencing the voices in your head; clarifying your intended audience; considering the experience of your readers; using conflicting feedback to clarify your intentions.

- Make sure that writers actually have important decisions to make when they write.

- Afford writers regular opportunities to write with their own intentions in mind.

- Help writers to find and create their own topics.

- Assist children as they identify, choose, fuse, and create genres that best carry the weight of their intended meanings.

- Help students find prewriting strategies that work for them; not every writer finds the same graphic organizer helpful, and some writers never find any graphic organizer useful.

- Allow students to decide when to develop an idea or piece of writing and when to move onto something new.

- Support children in identifying and understanding their intended readers in ways that don't create paralyzing self-consciousness.

- Help children ignore audience when needed.

- Reflect decisions and revisions to be made back on the writer's intention.

- Set up opportunities for students to share their texts with a variety of readers, not to grade or score the texts, but to articulate the effects of writers' choices in their experiences of reading.

- Help writers clarify their intentions based on a reader's experience.

- Ask questions about the text in terms of decision making and intention.

- Assist writers in sorting through sometimes-conflicting feedback to find and act on what is useful.

- Be willing *sometimes* to allow the child's intention for a writing project to trump yours.

Coda: What's It All For, Anyway?

It seems stupidly simple when I say it: teaching and writing and assessment are all about people who live and work together and who try to understand and help each other. In a society that strives to practice democracy, inclusion, and equity, this should have nothing to do with hierarchies and the scales that generate them. It should have nothing to do with control or alienation or the dismissal of experience. It should have nothing to do with winners and losers.

Instead, it's about a simple moment between two people. It's hard to see with all the technical jargon and mechanized systems, all the scales and judgement, all the noise and pressure in the way. If you're able to hold all that aside for a moment, you'll see it. It's just you, a human being who is also a teacher and a reader, who is also someone's child, someone's friend, someone's neighbor, and perhaps someone's parent. And it's your student, a human being who is also someone's child, someone's friend, someone's neighbor, and perhaps someone's parent, now or in the future. And within and between us is language. Will we be open to the experience? To each other?

References

Anson, C., ed. 1989. *Writing and Response: Theory, Practice, and Research*. Urbana, IL: NCTE.

Anson, C., et al. 2012. "Big Rubrics and Weird Genres: The Futility of Using Generic Assessment Tools Across Diverse Instructional Contexts." *The Journal of Writing Assessment* 5 (1): 4 June.

Atwell, N. 2007. *The Reading Zone: How to Help Kids Become Skilled, Passionate, Habitual, Critical Readers*. New York: Scholastic.

Black, E. 2012. *War Against the Weak: Eugenics and America's Campaign to Create a Master Race*. Washington, DC: Dialog Press.

Brophy, J. 2005. "Goal Theorists Should Move on from Performance Goals." *Educational Psychologist* 40 (3): 167–76.

Butler, R. 1987. "Task-Involving and Ego-Involving Properties of Evaluation: Effects of Different Feedback Conditions on Motivational Perceptions, Interest, and Performance." *Journal of Educational Psychology* 79 (4): 474–82.

Callahan, M. 2015. "The Brutal Secrets Behind 'The Biggest Loser.'" *New York Post*, January 18. http://nypost.com/2015/01/18/contestant-reveals-the-brutal-secrets-of-the- biggest-loser/.

Callahan, R. 1962. *Education and the Cult of Efficiency: A Study of the Social Forces That Have Shaped the Administration of the Public Schools*. Chicago: University of Chicago Press.

Cattell, R. B. 1997. "Open Letter to the APA." December 13. www.cattell.net/devon /openletter.htm.

Chaplin, Charlie. 1936. "Modern Times." Film. Charles Chaplin Productions.

Chomsky, N. 2000. *New Horizons in the Study of Language and Mind*. Cambridge, UK: Cambridge University Press.

Chomsky, N., and M. Kasenbacher. 2012. "Work, Learning, and Freedom." *New Left Project*, December 24. www.newleftproject.org/index.php/site/article_comments /work_learning_and_freedom.

Christensen, L. 2004–2005. "Moving Beyond Judgment." *Rethinking Schools* 19 (2): 33–37.

Cohler, B., and P. Hammack. 2006. "Making a Gay Identity: Life Story and the Construction of a Coherent Self." *Identity and Story: Creating Self in Narrative,* edited by Daniel McAdams, Ruthellen Josselson, and Amia Lieblich. Washington, DC: American Psychological Association.

"2013 College-Bound Seniors: Total Group Profile Report." (2013) *College Board.* http://media.collegeboard.com/digitalServices/pdf/research/2013/TotalGroup-2013.pdf.

Collins, S. 2008. The Hunger Games. New York: Scholastic.

Connors, R., and A. Lunsford. 1993. "Teachers' Rhetorical Comments on Student Papers." *College Composition and Communication.* 44 (2): 200–223.

Culham, R. 2006. *100 Trait-Specific Comments: A Quick Guide to Giving Constructive Feedback on Student Writing.* New York: Scholastic.

Dahl, R. 1980. *The Twits.* Illustrated by Quentin Blake. London, UK: Jonathan Cape Publishers.

Daiker, D. 1989. "Learning to Praise." In *Writing and Response,* edited by Chris Anson, 103–13. Urbana, IL: NCTE.

Darnon, C., et al. 2008. "Toward a Clarification of the Effects of Achievement Goals." *Revue International de Psychologie Sociale* 21 (1): 5–18.

Dewey, J. 1938. *Experience and Education.* West Lafayette, IN: Kappa Delta Pi.

Diederich, P., J. French, and S. Carlton. 1961. "Factors in Judgments of Writing Ability." *Educational Testing Service Research Bulletin* 61: 15.

Douglass, F. 1845. *Narrative of the Life of Frederick Douglass, an American Slave.* Boston: Anti-Slavery Office.

Dweck, C. 1999. *Self-Theories: Their Role in Motivation, Personality and Development.* Philadelphia: Taylor and Francis/Psychology Press.

———. 2006. *Mindset.* New York: Random House.

Dyer, K. 2015. "Use Formative Assessment as Your Classroom Fitbit." Formative Assessment. *Teach. Learn. Grow. The Education Blog.* Northwest Evaluation Association. September 24. https://www.nwea.org/blog/2015/use-formative-assessment-as-your-classroom-fitbit/.

Elbow, P. 1973. *Writing Without Teachers.* Oxford: Oxford University Press.

———. 1987. "Closing My Eyes as I Speak: An Argument for Ignoring Audience." *College English* 49 (1): 50–69.

———. 2000. *Everyone Can Write: Essays Toward a Hopeful Version of Teaching Theory of Writing and Teaching Writing.* New York: Oxford University Press.

Elbow, P. (cowritten with Jane Danielewicz). 2008. "A Unilateral Grading Contract to Improve Learning and Teaching." English Department Faculty Publication Series. http://scholarworks.umass.edu/eng_faculty_pubs/3.

Elbow, P., and P. Belanoff. 1989. *Sharing and Responding.* New York: Random House.

Elliot, N. 2005. *On a Scale: A Social History of Writing Assessment in America.* New York: Peter Lang.

Farley, T. 2009. *Making the Grades: My Misadventures in the Standardized Testing Industry.* San Francisco, CA: Berrett-Koehler.

Faughnder, R. 2014. "TV ratings: 'Biggest Loser' finale down from last year; CBS wins." *LATimes.* February 5. www.latimes.com/entertainment/envelope/cotown/la-et-ct-tv-ratings-biggest-loser-finale-down-from-last-year-20140205-story.html.

Franklin, N. 2011. "Northwest Noir: Dial AMC for Murder." *The New Yorker.* May 9. http://www.newyorker.com/magazine/2011/05/09/northwest-noir.

Gallagher, C., and E. Turley. 2012. *Our Better Judgement: Teacher Leadership in Assessment.* Urbana, IL: NCTE.

Gallagher, K. 2009. *Readicide: How Schools Are Killing Reading and What You Can Do About It.* Portland, ME: Stenhouse.

George, J. C. 1972. *Julie of the Wolves.* New York: HarperTrophy.

Gilson, D., and C. Perot. 2011. "It's the Inequality, Stupid." *Mother Jones.* March/April. http://www.motherjones.com/politics/2011/02/income-inequality-in-america-chart-graph/.

Good, R. H., and R. A. Kaminski. (Eds.). 2002. *Dynamic Indicators of Basic Early Literacy Skills,* 6th ed. Eugene, OR: Institute for the Development of Educational Achievement. https://dibels.uoregon.edu.

Gottfredson, L. 1994. "Mainstream Science on Intelligence." *Wall Street Journal.* December 13 A:18.

Gould, S. J. 1981. *The Mismeasure of Man.* New York: W. W. Norton.

Hagopian, J., ed. 2014. *More Than a Score: The New Uprising Against High-Stakes Testing.* Chicago, IL: Haymarket Books.

Hart, R. et al. 2015. "Student Testing in America's Great City Schools: An Inventory and Preliminary Analysis." Council of the Great City Schools. https://www.cgcs.org/cms/lib/DC00001581/Centricity/Domain/87/Testing%20Report.pdf.

Haswell, J. and R. Haswell. 2010. *Authoring: An Essay for the English Profession on Potentiality and Singularity.* Logan, UT: Utah State University Press.

Herbert, B. 1994. "In America; Throwing a Curve." *New York Times.* October 26. www.nytimes.com/1994/10/26/opinion/in-america-throwing-a-curve.html.

Herrnstein, R., and C. Murray. 1994. *The Bell Curve: Intelligence and Class Structure in American Life.* New York: Free Press.

Holleyman, S. 1993. *Mona the Brilliant.* New York: Doubleday Books for Young Readers.

Huxley, A. 1932. *Brave New World.* London: Chatto and Windus.

Jones, P. 2009. "From 'External Speech' to 'Inner' Speech in Vygotsky: A Critical Appraisal and Fresh Perspectives." *Language & Communication* 29: 166–81.

King, S. 2000. *On Writing: A Memoir of the Craft.* New York: Scribner.

Kittle, P. 2013. *Book Love: Developing Depth, Stamina, and Passion in Adolescent Readers.* Portsmouth, NH: Heinemann.

Kohn, A. 1993. *Punished by Rewards: The Trouble with Gold Stars, Incentive Plans, A's, Praise, and Other Bribes.* Boston: Houghton Mifflin.

———. 1999. *The Schools Our Children Deserve.* Boston: Houghton Mifflin.

Kolata, G. 2016. "After 'The Biggest Loser,' Their Bodies Fought to Regain Weight." *New York Times.* May 2, 2016. www.nytimes.com/2016/05/02/health/biggest-loser -weight-loss.html?_r=0.

Lamott, A. 1994. *Bird by Bird: Some Instructions on Writing and Life.* New York: Anchor Books.

Lynne, P. 2004. *Coming to Terms: A Theory of Writing Assessment.* Logan, UT: Utah State University Press.

McAdams, D. 1988. *Power, Intimacy, and the Life Story: Personological Inquiries into Identity.* New York: Guilford Press.

———.2006. "The Role of Narrative in Personality Psychology Today." *Narrative Inquiry* 16 (1). https://www.sesp.northwestern.edu/docs/publications/1049432884490 a09930cdc3.pdf.

McAdams, D., R. Josselson, and A. Lieblich. 2006. "Introduction." In *Identity and Story: Creating Self in Narrative,* edited by Daniel McAdams, Ruthellen Josselson, and Amia Lieblich. Washington, DC: American Psychological Association.

McCloskey, R. 1976. *One Morning in Maine.* New York: Puffin Books.

McLoyd, V. 1979. "The Effects of Extrinsic Rewards of Differential Value on High and Low Intrinsic Interest." *Child Development* 50 (4): 1010–19.

McLuhan, M. 1994. *Understanding Media: The Extensions of Man*. Boston: MIT Press.

Mischel, W. 2004. "Toward an Integrative Science of the Person." *Annual Review of Psychology* 55: 1–22.

Molnar, M. 2017. "Formative Assessments Go Digital." *Education Week*. May 24: 28–31.

Morin, A. 2012. "Inner Speech." In *Encyclopedia of Human Behavior*, edited by W. Hirstein. 436–43. New York: Elsevier.

Moss, C., S. Brookhart, and B. Long. 2011. "Knowing Your Learning Target." *Educational Leadership* 68 (6): 66–69.

Murray, D. 1970. "The Interior View of Composing: One Writer's Philosophy of Composition." *College Composition and Communication* 21: 21–6.

———. 1982. "Teaching the Other Self: The Writer's First Reader." *College Composition and Communication* 33: 140–47.

Newkirk, T. 2000. "Misreading Masculinity: Speculations on the Great Gender Gap in Writing." *Language Arts* 77 (4): 294–300.

———. 2005. *The School Essay Manifesto: Reclaiming the Essay for Students and Teachers*. Shoreham, VT: Discover Writing.

———. 2012. *The Art of Slow Reading: Six Time-Honored Practices for Engagement*. Portsmouth, NH: Heinemann.

Olsen, M. A., and F. Swineford. 1953. "Reliability and Validity of an Interlinear Test of Writing Ability." *Educational Testing Service Research Bulletin* 53–09:i-6.

Oomen, A. M. 2006. *House of Fields: Memories of a Rural Education*. Detroit, MI: Wayne State University Press.

Paulsen, G. 1987. *Hatchet*. New York: Scholastic.

Paulsen, G. 1989. *The Winter Room*. New York: Yearling.

Perez-Pena, R. 2014. "Best, Brightest, and Rejected: Elite Colleges Turn Away Up to 95%." *New York Times*. April 8. https://www.nytimes.com/2014/04/09/us/led-by -stanfords-5-top-colleges-acceptance-rates-hit-new-lows.html?_r=0.

Pink, D. 2009. *Drive: The Surprising Truth About What Motivates Us*. New York: Riverhead Books.

Plato. 2001. *The Republic*. Millis, MA: Agora Publications.

Pulfrey, C., et al. 2011. "Why Grades Engender Performance-Avoidance Goals: The Mediating Role of Autonomous Motivation." *Journal of Educational Psychology* 103: 683–700.

Ray, K. W. 2006. "What Are You Thinking?" *Educational Leadership* 64 (2): 58–62.

———. 2010. *In Pictures and In Words: Teaching the Qualities of Good Writing Through Illustration Study*. Portsmouth, NH: Heinemann.

Romano, T. 2008. *Zigzag: A Life of Reading and Writing, Teaching and Learning*. Portsmouth, NH: Heinemann.

Rubenstein, R. 2012. "An Interview with Todd Farley." *Diane Ravitch's Blog*. December 27. https://dianeravitch.net/2012/12/27/11990/.

Ryan, R., and E. Deci. 1985. *Intrinsic Motivation and Self-Determination in Human Behavior*. New York: Kluwer Academic/Plenum Publishers.

———. 2000. "Intrinsic and Extrinsic Motivators: Classic Definitions and New Directions." *Contemporary Educational Psychology* 25: 54–67.

Sacks, O. 1989. *Seeing Voices: A Journey Into the World of the Deaf*. Berkley, CA: University of California Press.

Seneca, L. A. *Moral Epistles* (Letter). Translated by Richard M. Gunmere. The Loeb Classical Library. Cambridge, MA: Harvard University Press, 1917–25. 3 vols.: Volume I.

Serrano, R. A. 2015. "Obama Proposes Capping Standardized Testing at 2% of Classroom Time." *LATimes*. October 24. www.latimes.com/local/education/la-na -obama-testing-policy-20151024-story.html.

"Setting Measures of Academic Progress Goals." 2010. Youtube. 5:27. May 6. https:// www.youtube.com/watch?v=MVLwu6uQK2I.

Shaughnessy, M. 1977. *Errors and Expectations*. Oxford: Oxford University Press.

Snicket, L. 1999. *The Bad Beginning: or, Orphans!* (A Series of Unfortunate Events No. 1). New York: HarperTrophy.

Spandel, V. 2006. "In Defense of Rubrics." *English Journal* 96 (1): 19–22.

Stiggins, R. 2005. "From Formative Assessment to Assessment FOR Learning: A Path to Success in Standards-Based Schools." *Phi Delta Kappan* 87 (4): 324–28.

Stiggins, R., and J. Chapuis. 2012. *An Introduction to Student-Involved Assessment FOR Learning*, 6th ed. Boston, MA: Pearson.

Stiglitz, J. 2011. "Of the 1%, By the 1%, For the 1%." *Vanity Fair.* May. http://www .vanityfair.com/news/2011/05/top-one-percent-201105.

Strauss, V. 2013. "Pearson Criticized for Finding Test Essay Scorers on Craigslist." *Washington Post* Answer Sheet. January 16.

Taylor, F. 1911. *The Principles of Scientific Management.* New York: Harper & Brothers.

Thompson, T. 2009. "6 Traits." *English Companion Ning.* April 1.http://englishcom- panion.ning.com

Urdan, T. 2001. "Contextual Influences on Motivation and Performance: An Examination of Achievement Goal Structures." In *Student Motivation,* edited by Salilil, F., Chiu, C.Y.,Hong, Y.Y. (eds). 171–201. New York: Kluwer Academic/Plenum Publishers.

Vygotsky, L. 1986. In *Thought and Language,* edited by A. Kozulin. Cambridge, MA: MIT Press.

Winner, L. 2000. "Do Artifacts Have Politics?" In *Technology, Organizations and Innovation: Theories, Concepts and Paradigms,* edited by I. McLoughlin, D. Preece, and P. Dawson, 531–44. London: Routledge.

Wilson, M. 2006. *Rethinking Rubrics in Writing Assessment.* Portsmouth, NH: Heinemann.

———. 2007. "Why I Won't Be Using Rubrics to Respond to Students' Writing." *English Journal* 96 (4): 62–66.

———. 2007b. "The View from Somewhere." *Educational Leadership* 65 (4): 76–80.

———. 2009. "Responsive Writing Assessment." *Educational Leadership* 67 (3): 58–62.

———. 2010. "There Are a Lot of Really Bad Teachers Out There." *Phi Delta Kappan* 92 (2): 51–55.

———. 2013. "Writing Assessment's 'Debilitating Inheritance': Behaviorism's Dismissal of Experience." PhD diss, University of New Hampshire.

Winfield, A. 2007. *Eugenics and Education in America: Institutionalized Racism and the Implications of History, Ideology, and Memory.* New York: Peter Lang.

Yerkes, R., and C. Yoakum, eds. 1920. *Army Mental Tests.* New York: Henry Holt.

Zenderland, Leila. 2001. *Measuring Minds: Henry Herbert Goddard and the Origins of American Intelligence Testing.* Cambridge: Cambridge University Press.

Index